My
ILLUSION
—— *of* ——
NORMAL

THE PECULIAR CASE
OF JEAN STEVENS

TOM CARMAN

"It may be normal, darling; but I'd rather be natural."

— Truman Capote, Breakfast at Tiffany's

To my parents, wife and Michael, Sarah, Zeb, Dominic, and Terence

Their positive support and positive influence are what brought my efforts to fruition. A special thank you to my wife, Cammy, and our children for their understanding of my absence during many holidays, sporting events and countless meals. More importantly, to God who has blessed me with a fruitful life and continues to bless me daily, not only with the ability to be mindful but also the desire to offer hope and change to others.

AUTHOR

THOMAS M. CARMAN

This book is dedicated to the memory of Jean Lucille Stevens,
a loving sister, a good wife, and a dear friend.

APRIL 13, 1919 – FEBRUARY 29, 2012

MY FRIEND JEAN.

PHOTO BY THOMAS M. CARMAN

My Illusion of Normal
Copyright © 2024 by Tom Carman. All rights reserved.

MINDSTIR MEDIA

Published by MindStir Media, LLC
45 Lafayette Rd | Suite 181| North Hampton, NH 03862 | USA
1.800.767.0531 | www.mindstirmedia.com

Printed in the United States of America.
ISBN-13: 978-1-962987-58-5

TABLE OF CONTENTS

ACKNOWLEDGMENTS

This book results from years of interaction with families, colleagues, local, state, federal agencies, fire and EMS agencies. Those whom I wish to acknowledge for their assistance in the Jean Stevens case are:

- Pennsylvania State Police
- Bradford County District Attorney's office
- Honorable Judge Beirne who received my Petition for Exhumation and who set forth the Order of Exhumation.
- Dr. Jeff D Aronsohn D.D.S. who was instrumental in positively identifying the remains of James and June Stevens.
- Bradford County Area Agency on Aging
- The former Towanda Memorial Hospital EMS
- The American Board of Medicolegal Death Investigators
- American College of Forensic Examiners Institute
- Pennsylvania Coroner's Association.
- Forensic Pathologist Dr. James Terzian and Dr. Robert Stopphacher for their continued support and guidance.

INTRODUCTION

My name is Tom Carman. I am a retired medicolegal death investigator. I am now a born-again Christian who dedicates my life to serving our Lord. This book is the result of over 20 years of experience in the field of medicolegal death investigation. Being directly involved with over 2,000 death investigations, I have had the opportunity to work with many agencies, including county, state, and federal. I have also had the opportunity to meet many families, see the lifestyle, and hear the ideology of hundreds.

I have been deemed an expert in the field of death investigation by the Court of Common Pleas, but else wise, I am a simple man with a love for Christ and a desire to bring others to the Lord by offering hope and lived experience.

It would be within a short period of time that I would come to the realization that people are as unique as many of the cases themselves. This uniqueness often brings light to a very dark scenario. This light brings about explanation, family reunion, and at most times, understanding. Most times meaning that things are not always completely understood. In fact, both families and investigators are occasionally left with an absence of reason and understanding. It is not death we mourn, but the reasoning behind it.

In those respective cases where there is discovery of understanding and etiology, I'm reminded of Matthew 4:16, "The people living in darkness have seen a great light; on those living in the land of the shadow of death a light has dawned."

From scripture, Isaiah speaks in a prophetic style. A simple synopsis in a place of the overspreading of spiritual darkness both knowledge and holiness came about them from understanding the principles of Christ. Likewise, with death (darkness), understanding can come about when we possess an open mind and systematically approach each investigation. On the other hand, the inevitability of death is highly overwhelming. Some people in their old age fear death. But, little do they know, fear has nothing to do with death, for it is death that fears nothing. People fear the process of death rather than death itself. As a result, there's a potential for them to experience the terror of death consciously. At the core of the fear of death is the fear of destruction, which refers to the extinction of mind, spirit, and soul and the destruction of the body- that is nonexistent.

I have discovered throughout my career that what I once interpreted as normalcy was grossly misunderstood. I have learned that lifestyles greatly vary from individual to individual, situation to situation, and ideology to ideology. A "normal situation" and "normal behavior" are relative to any given individual in any given environment. With an open, non-judgmental mind, and a desire to seek facts, the truth will prevail regardless of societal or cultural norms and/or personal beliefs.

The compilation of case notes described within this book will illustrate human action, emotion, and ideology of what these decedents considered to be normal. Perhaps most arguably, normal is no more than fallacy. In no way are any of these cases mentioned intended to be judgmental, disrespectful, or a form of embarrassment to the decedent, family members, friends, or associates. As you read these stories, it is crucial to remember Romans 3:23, "For all have sinned and fall short of the glory of God."

For the exception of Jean Stevens and related investigative information pertaining to this case, all other cases mentioned within this book have been changed for the protection of both the dead and the living. These changes include names, locations and dates. The names and locations used in these cases are purely fictitious and in no uncertain terms represent the factual identity of the person, actual date, or town in which these incidents occurred.

This book does however contain a factual, behind-the-scene look into the case of Jean Stevens. A case that would change my life, both professionally and personally, forever. Together, Jean and I learned from each other. It is with expressed consent and expectation by Jean that her story be told. This case is particularly of interest since it caters to the topic of death and life and how loneliness brings havoc in our normally functioning life. Social isolation can drive people to do things they wouldn't usually consider doing. Humans are conflicted about their mortality and that of their kin and friends. Regardless of how a person has lived, they're bound to fall on their knees when they experience abandonment and social seclusion. The denial of death is an essential factor in knowing how and why relationships with other social beings are fundamentally exploitative and harmful. Since death separates one being from the other, the feeling of never meeting the one that is gone is excruciating. Separation drives a person crazy and instills a pursuit of meeting the ones that are gone. Norman Cousins says, "Death is not the greatest loss in life. The greatest loss is what dies inside us while we live." Since humans live their lives socializing and networking, the loss of special moments upon someone's death makes them feel aloof and heartbroken. Reminiscence of priceless memories shared with the deceased leaves an unfillable void in one's heart.

Monophobia, which refers to the fear of being lonely at some point in time in the future also triggers feelings of loneliness and goes to the extent of mania. Such feelings are commonly seen within old age groups since they consider that being old jeopardizes their identity and personality. They are of the view that age-related illnesses, loss of network of friends, difficulty communicating, and death of a spouse or a loved one may make them weak, stubborn, and worse – alone. Their intuition tells them that they are no longer helpful to society and thus feel trapped in destructive thoughts involving death and isolation.

Chapter 1

SHE LOVES ME.
SHE LOVES ME NOT

In the beginning, there was a man named Adam and a woman named Eve. After being beautifully created, together, they found themselves present within the Garden of Eden. There were plenty of fruitful trees, animals, and plants to eat throughout. In the center of the garden was a tree of life, a tree of knowledge - knowledge of both good and evil. God gave Adam and Eve but one commandment, do not eat from this tree, or you shall surely die.

Genesis 2:16-17, "And the Lord God commanded the man, saying, of every tree of the garden thou mayest freely eat: But of the tree of the knowledge of good and evil, thou shalt not eat of it: for in the day that thou eatest thereof thou shalt surely die."

Shortly after that came a serpent who convinced Eve to eat the apple from this forbidden tree, followed by Eve convincing Adam to partake as well. This would be the first deception presented to mankind by the serpent - the evil one. At this very moment, mankind became sinful. Satan now had control over earth; man would become fallible with that, came death.

Sounds like the plot of a horror film, doesn't it? It did for me for many of my younger years. This concept of a God, a devil, Heaven, and hell was overwhelming and honestly too much for my young developing brain to comprehend. The phenomenon always stuns the mind and becomes incomprehensible. I heard about God from an early age but also about Santa, the Easter Bunny, and the Tooth Fairy. A man, woman, apple, and snake (serpent), were almost more challenging to accept than the others.

I loved the idea of a superior being out there somewhere looking after me. I would hold on to this hope right up until the point in my life when I realized many years later that it wasn't just an idea but the truth. It is true how the omnipotence of God extends over the entire universe and how the matters concerning life, death, angels, and devils have so much more significance to it than just being a few topics discussed in the Holy books.

I admit, initially, I wasn't a born-again Christian, and I certainly didn't understand death. I wouldn't reach that point until many years later in life. If I'm going to be totally honest with you, when I first pursued a position within the coroner's office in 1999 it was primarily to better understand death.

Being exposed to many deaths in my youth and teenage years raised many questions. Questions that I knew could only be answered by facing death head-on. If I couldn't understand death, I would strive to understand its complex methods. Death had slowly seeped into my daily thoughts. I had and remain with the absolute knowledge to this day that death will someday turn its gaze upon me. The question became, when my time comes would I fear death or view it as an old friend? No one knows. The only thing we know is that life is ephemeral while death is inevitable. However, we as humans tend to confuse the latter with one another and think of life as something that will exist for eons and that death only comes to the old. We are not wrong but are wronged. Humans cannot seem to untie the blindfolds which would make them see the reality and the truth of life, no matter how bitter.

I may not have been a great man of faith and certainly didn't walk by it when I was younger, but I did believe in love. I may not have understood its definition, but I certainly knew the associated feelings – the connection, the stomach butterflies, the commitment, the aroma, the sensual touch, the essence of true love. Do you remember your first true love and that feeling of being on top of the world? Wow, and how about that first kiss? Yes, I remember my first true love. I remember the overpowering sensation of happiness and that emotional connection. Love itself is beautiful. It is the mysterious force that binds people to those around them. It has infinite forms, and each of the forms never stays the same for long. Love is constantly evolving and changing. My own experience with love comes in many forms. I love many people and many things, all in different ways. Love to me is one of the purest things in the world. People who hate and do not love are certainly not from us. Love is necessary to function in the world we live in.

For me, nothing else much mattered. I now not only had something in common with my social circle, but I also had a best friend—someone to go to the dances, movies, pool hall, and parties with. Yes, life was good, and very little meant more.

Suddenly my heart skipped a beat. I became nauseated and depressed. The devastating news came crashing down on me like pearls from a broken necklace cascading down only to hit the floor and turn into an ugly, gooey mess. The beauty was gone.

"I'm breaking up with you. I have found someone else."

"Hold on, what, wait, this can't be happening. We are in love. Why?"

The somber realization that life, as I knew it, had just changed dramatically was never more prevalent. I now must face my friends and continue to act happy when I couldn't even talk about this. Hold on; I can't face my friends like this! I can't have them busting my chops. Furthermore, how am I going to explain this deep funk I'm in? I have pride. I'm a man, damn it!

Okay, there must be a way to pull this off. How can I downplay this funk I'm in. All these crazy emotions, tears, and loss of interest in my daily routine. What am I going to do? I could care less if I lived or died.

This would be my first true experience with sincere prayer, even though I didn't understand to who I was praying. It was either pray or potentially kill myself with this intense depression in which I drowned myself. But prayers, I believe, heal the most pained hearts. The Lord is close to the brokenhearted and saves those who are crushed in spirit.

I'm guessing you can relate to a similar event in your life where you shared these same temporary emotions only to heal and move forward. Question, what if you didn't heal? What if you didn't get through it? What if you didn't allow time to do what it does best, heal?

To get stuck in a loop of countless miseries is even worse. This repetitive cycle of depression traps you within and doesn't let you escape the intrusive thoughts. Loneliness is one of its aspects. It can make things worse for you and your sanity in the long run. During the early Monday morning hours on a cool but sunny day in November, I received a telephone call. This call was from the 911 Center, which advised that they had an incident that required my response. Nothing new, really. This is typical. Consequently, it was just another day in my mind of performing the role of Coroner.

Traveling along an asphalt roadway in a very rural setting, it seemed as though I would never arrive on location. This is not uncommon due to the geographical size of our county, predominately being what was once farmlands. The area is beautiful but comes with the price tag of an extended travel time, being over an hour from county line to county line.

Finally, I arrived at the location. The driveway is a mixture of dirt and stone neatly compacted in place. I find that it is a long driveway with the residence itself sitting a bit uphill. In the driveway sit a couple of police cruisers and two or three private vehicles, presumably belonging to the residents of the home.

The house itself is a beautiful private two-story home. The shingled roof highlights the property. The design is a traditional split-level home, vinyl siding with neatly trimmed windows combined with this beautiful roof which truly brings this property to life. The landscaping surrounding the entire front facade is tidy, although being November in Pennsylvania, there isn't much to admire as far as flowers and blooms. I can only imagine how colorful it is during the spring The landscape looks pristine, and the tranquility makes staying there worthwhile.

There's a concrete sidewalk that leads to the front door. The sunshine assures it's free of snow and ice, making it risk-free from slipping to the ground. This is not always the case in my line of work. I can't begin to tell you how often I have slipped and fallen while walking on or over something during the winter months.

Upon opening the front door, I am greeted by my fellow friends from the patrol unit of the state police. Criminal Investigator Nick Gonzales is reportedly on his way. A crime scene log had been established, and I signed in. This is a common practice in any of our scenes. We log in who we are, what agency we're from, and the time of anyone entering our crime scene. I say "crime scene" because everything is considered a crime scene until we prove otherwise.

Standing in the doorway, ready to be briefed on the situation, I hear a female crying hysterically in the background. It's evident due to the hysteria coming from an adjoining room that this is someone very close to the victim. How close and whom I'm not aware of at this point.

Shortly after, I am approached by this female who obviously is emotionally distraught. I quickly realize that she is in her 40s and is the mother of whoever has passed. Sadly, I now know that our victim must be of a young age.

The female identifies herself as Barbara Rakowski, and in a trembling voice, states, "I am his mother." I express my sincerest condolences for her loss. This is one of the most critical parts of starting a dialogue with anyone who has just lost someone they love. In my mind, compassion is step one in gaining trust, understanding, and knowledge in any given scenario where the interviewee is not the suspect.

After expressing my care and concern, I kindly asked Ms. Rakowski to wait in the kitchen, explaining that I would be back to talk with her once we gathered some information pertaining to the scene. She politely complies and returns to the kitchen.

Prior to starting our processing of the scene, a male within the same age group now approached me. The male introduces himself as Donald Rakowski, the father of the victim. Mr. Rakowski presents in pajamas and barefoot and is obviously emotionally distraught by the situation. His hands are trembling, and his eyes reveal a deepened sadness. The glasses on his face have spots from the countless tears he shed – still wet making their presence known like the deep pain seethed into the pits of the hearts of the mother and father of the dead. Offering my condolences, I asked Mr. Rakowski to wait with his wife in the kitchen.

About this time, Trooper Nick Gonzales arrives at the location and walks through the door. We quickly connect, and Nick signs the crime log. After discussing that both Mr. and Mrs. Rakowski are present, we collectively decided that we would initiate a preliminary interview with both parents before processing the scene.

Our hope was that this would be comforting to Mr. and Mrs. Rakowski and possibly assist in convincing them to go to a relative's home or at least a neighboring home while we process the scene.

Processing any given scene can appear to be aggressive and is certainly methodical. This can be very intimidating to family members.

With this in mind, we made our way into the kitchen where Mr. & Mrs. Rakowski were present, bent over each other as if a pivotal piece of their puzzle had been snatched from them. Throughout the interview, we would learn that the victim is Carter Rakowski, a white male, 15 years of age, and is indeed the son of Mr. and Mrs. Rakowski. We would gain additional information about Carter that would assist with what we call victimology.

Carter was not only an "A" student but also very active in sports. We learned that he was a well-liked teenager who was respected by both his classmates and teachers.

Carter loved the outdoors, especially hunting, which is a favorite hobby of many of our youth within our county. We would also learn that Carter was gainfully employed at a local retail shop, working after school hours and occasionally on the weekend. For all intents and purposes, Carter was a well-rounded, well-liked, and what would be deemed a normal teen as far as a profile perspective.

These initial few minutes were crucial in discovering an initial profile of Carter. Victimology is a great tool that provides us the ability to have a better understanding of whomever we are dealing with. For example, we now know we are dealing with a younger male, smart, physically fit, mindful of nature, and has a basic understanding of weapons. This is crucial information to learn when dealing with any unnatural death.

Further conversation with Mr. and Mrs. Rakowski would reveal that Carter is righthanded and has no significant past medical history. However, they offer that Carter, with no official medical diagnosis does suffer from depression. Furthermore, Carter has had a past suicidal ideology which he had generically mentioned to his parents. Mr. and Mrs. Rakowski clearly state that Carter has never actually attempted suicide, almost in a minimizing fashion, meaning that it was just talk. In fact, they state it was more of an idle threat scenario. However, in our world, this is red flag number #1.

With no intended disrespect, if suicidal ideology is verbalized, this should not be taken lightly or brushed under the rug. This is a mind that has traveled to a dark place. Regardless of circumstance, these expressed words can be long-lasting and haunting if left ignored. People should never ignore suicidal tendencies. These escalate into something dangerous and eventually result in people losing their lives. Sometimes verbalized responses speak more than the actions themselves. Verbalized suicidal responses may also be treated to prevent suicides from happening altogether.

Honestly, I believe that any one of us with life experience can relate to the fact that life can surely be a bit depressing and overwhelming at times. In fact, learning Carter's history wasn't necessarily surprising, considering that a great portion of our society suffers from depression of various forms, including our youth. The key is Carter verbalized this ideology. The first step is more than likely subconsciously asking for help. I find this very concerning, considering that although many suffer from depression, now we have a young man who is thinking of an end. In essence, he is beginning to write the final chapter in his book of life.

Mr. and Mrs. Rakowski proceed to tell us that Carter is not medicated but does seek counseling on a semi-regular basis. Again, not necessarily concerning but does place emphasis on the severity of his mental health. It is not uncommon to find that young adults are not medicated for depression due to the common side effects that can occur with children and older teens, especially the potential risk of further suicidal ideology and the strong likelihood of sexual performance difficulty.

We learn that Carter is a heterosexual and has had past girlfriends. Mr. and Mrs. Rakowski attempt to be forthright with any past relationships they are aware of. They informed us that he was friends with an older female named Kelly, who is a waitress at a local eating establishment.

Mr. and Mrs. Rakowski state that Carter is an intelligent boy who is a perfectionist, especially pertaining to his school grades. They go on to say, Carter has been upset recently over not achieving an "A" in his calculus class. Carter views less than an "A" in any given subject as a personal failure.

In reviewing the prior 24 hours of activity with Mr. and Mrs. Rakowski. we learn from Mr. Rakowski that both he and Carter had been out hunting yesterday. This is something they have in common and find enjoyment in doing together. Upon returning home, Carter took his weapon to his room to properly clean it. Mr. Rakowski gives no impression that yesterday was anything but normal, but stated that he spent more time than usual in his room.

Mr. Rakowski states that he awoke this a.m. and went downstairs to cook breakfast at 06:00, adding that Carter was supposed to be up by 06:30 but did not come down. Mr. Rakowski stated that this was unusual, so he went upstairs to Carter's room, where he discovered the door was locked. Mr. Rakowski knocks on the door with no response. Alarmed, Mr. Rakowski then kicked the door in and discovered Carter's body. He screamed, waking Mrs. Rakowski, and she ran in.

Mrs. Rakowski is more open and informative. Honestly, we tend to see this frequently while investigating. Fathers tend to be more reserved and confidential, often not fully realizing that the minor details can be a major break in a case.

While Mr. Rakowski went to the coffeemaker to get a cup of coffee, Mrs. Rakowski enlightened us on a few things that would set the stage, filling in many of the unanswered questions. Mrs. Rakowski informed us that she has been really concerned about Carter these past few months. At this point, we knew the truth would prevail. A mother's love for a child and the light it brings about will always

MY ILLUSION of NORMAL

bring darkness to light, assuming the mother has no involvement in the death.

Mrs. Rakowski states that Carter ran away two weeks ago, taking one of the family vehicles, and drove to upstate New York. Within a few hours, Carter called Mrs. Rakowski, informing her he was sorry and was returning home. This was totally out of character for Carter but in our minds, this was red flag #2. We now have verbalized suicidal ideology and acting outside of normal 'Carter' character.

Mrs. Rakowski proceeds; Carter came down for dinner last evening but quickly returned to his room. Shortly thereafter, Carter returned downstairs to get a beverage. Mrs. Rakowski informed Carter that the family was going to play a game and asked if he would like to participate. Carter replied, "No." He thought he'd skip it and go back to his room. This was not like Carter. He loved games. Now we have red flag #3. Verbalized suicidal ideology, acting out of 'Carter' character, and now isolation. The big question that remains is WHY?

At 21:30 last evening, Mrs. Rakowski sent Carter a text asking if she had to worry about him tonight. He replied, "no." I have found that a mother's intuition is seldom wrong. Sadly, this would be Mrs. Rakowski's last conversation with her son.

Nick and I made our way out of the kitchen into the living room, looking around to assess the residence. The living room was very tidy and comfortable appearing. The walls hosted several family photographs. This would be the first time I would put a face to Carter. He was a handsome, healthy-looking, well-fit young man.

Displayed photographs revealed much love and family bond. This appeared to be a normal loving family with a healthy home. However, experience has taught me that a quality facade often does not necessarily depict the interior.

Now standing at the base of the stairs that lead upwards to the bedrooms, including Carter's, I heard a soft female voice ask, "May I talk to you?" Realizing this voice was directed at me, I turned and replied, "yes." Standing behind me was a female who identified herself as Carter's sister, Lindsey.

Lindsey proceeded to tell me that she thought we should know a couple of things. Trying to hold back tears, Lindsey tells me that Carter was more than just friends with Kelly. In fact, Carter and Kelly had been sexually involved in an intimate relationship for the past year. Lindsey goes on to say that two weeks ago, Kelly broke it off with Carter.

I immediately posed the question, "Do your parents know about this?" Lindsey replied, "no." Now darkness was continuing to turn to light. Lindsey proceeds to tell me that this was when Carter started cutting himself, but their parents did not know about it. I asked, "They don't know about Kelly or the cutting?" Carter makes the cutting marks on his legs so they can be covered with jeans. This is huge and clearly establishes red flag #4.

It's important to remember that cutting is a serious red flag not only for the investigation but also for any parent to be mindful. This type of self-injury is a harmful way to cope with emotional pain, intense anger and frustration. People who cut may not know better ways to get relief from emotional pain or pressure. People may also cut to express strong feelings of rage, sorrow, rejection, desperation, longing, or emptiness. When these emotions don't get expressed healthily, tension can build up – sometimes to a point where it seems almost unbearable. It's also important to note that self-injury may bring a momentary sense of calm and release of tension. It's generally followed by guilt and shame, which can actually worsen the depression. Through experience, I have found life-threatening injuries are usually not the intention. However, it can certainly present the possibility of more severe and even fatal self-aggressive actions down the road.

For investigative purposes, we differentiate self-cutting injuries from hesitation marks or injuries. Hesitation marks are periodically discovered with a traumatic suicide. This is where the actor gets a feel for the pain that's associated with the act they are about to perform. These injuries are fresh and blood-filled. Contrary to this, self-inflicted cutting marks or scars are generally the remnants of an ongoing form of self-punishment. These particular injuries present in varying degrees of healing.

I immediately ask Lindsey, "How old is Kelly?" Lindsey replies, "She is 20." Now I don't ask this to be nosey. I ask because there is a big difference between a developing 15-year-old male brain and a 20- year-old female brain. The maturity level alone can be great. Bottom line, we now have new facts and circumstances coming into our investigation. Consequently, Lindsey ends up being our best source of information.

Lindsey's crying continues, "You need to know that this was when Carter started smoking marijuana."

"Interesting," I replied. None of this was mentioned by your Mom and Dad. Lindsey replied with tear-filled eyes, "They aren't aware of it. Carter and I talked about a lot of things. He was my best friend." I momentarily rested my hand on her shoulder and thanked her for her honesty and concern for Carter.

Nick and I slowly start advancing upwards at the base of the stairs. The stairs are wooden and relatively quiet, with little to no squeaks. I remember the awkwardness of the quietness. The lack of natural sunlight while climbing the stairs only added to this eerie feeling.

Upon reaching the top step, it hit me – the abundant aroma of death combined with the stench of stale blood that I am accustomed to. This aroma is hard to explain. Simply put, unoxygenated, stagnant blood takes on a unique odor. Combined with the smell of death, you have a long-lasting, unique aroma that lingers in your sinuses for hours.

To our left was a full-sized bathroom. To our right were two additional bedrooms, both of which had open doors. The bedrooms appeared clean and tidy and presented no indication that any type of struggle or domestic disturbance had occurred. Straight ahead was Carter's bedroom.

Now came the time to open the door leading into his bedroom. There's evidence to support the statement made by Mr. Rakowski that he used forcible entry to gain entrance earlier. The wood had been cracked and damaged near the latch.

To my surprise, upon fully opening the door, I could hear music coming from a laptop present on a nightstand next to Carter's bed. There was blood splatter on the computer screen. Such a young man with an obvious old spirit present before me. Frankly, it was a little chilling – the remains of Carter before me and this CCR song playing repeatedly. It haunts me to this day. Every time I hear this song on the oldies station, it takes me back to Carter's bedroom.

Carter lays fully dressed upon the bed in a supine position (face up). His skin is pale and extremely cold. Sadly, what was left of Carter's skull was lying on the pillow. Blood, tissue, and bone fragments were scattered upon the bed, wall, floor, and ceiling. Along with Carter on the bed were two long rifles and a hand-written note covered with blood droplets. The note itself would reveal Carter's saddest, intimate, and final thoughts.

Discovered was the actual suicide note, portraying a young, heartbroken teenager—a teen who had so much passion and love for another. Suddenly the full realization of the power of love came full circle in my mind. Standing there in a momentary trance, I reflected upon 1 Corinthians 13:13, "So much faith, hope, and love abide, these three, but the greatest is love." When we think about it, faith and loving one another are the two critical components of Christianity, and Carter had both. I had to ask myself, what went wrong?

I must say placing Carter in a body bag was not an easy task. Finding myself reminiscing on my own past, knowing the pain associated with losing your first true love, produced a flood of brain emotions. However, the job must go on. As a Christian, I believe that the soul and body separate upon death, leaving behind only the shell of what once was.

Upon carrying Carter down the stairwell and placing him into the back of my vehicle for transport, I again heard the voice of Lindsey. "Mr. Carman, I need to ask you something." As I turned around to face this young woman, she asked, "Do you think my brother is going to hell?" At this very moment, I realized that her biggest concern was Carter's well-being and where his soul would spend eternity. I simply replied, "We serve a loving and forgiving Lord."

If I'm totally honest with you, Lindsey's voice stuck with me all day. Still troubled by this, I dove into some biblical research when I got home later that evening. Do you know, nowhere could I find in scripture where suicide was condemnation to hell? In fact, suicide is mentioned multiple times throughout the Bible, but nowhere does it state what happens to the spirit and soul of the individual. Two of the incidents of self-killing in the Bible exhibit a positive attitude toward suicide. Arguably, the author of the Gospel of Matthew intends the reader to interpret the disciple Judas's hanging as an act of remorse. Judas repents (metamelētheis) and returns the blood money that he received for turning Jesus over to the authorities who executed him (Matt 27:3). Judas acknowledges that he has "sinned in betraying innocent blood" (Matt 27:4). His suicide may be interpreted as an act of atonement because he himself carries out the penalty laid down in the Hebrew Bible for taking a life: "no expiation can be made for the land, for the blood that is shed in it, except by the blood of him who shed it" (Num 35:33; see also Lev 24:17). There is no hint of condemnation of Judas's self-killing in Matthew. If anything, it is a solution to his guilt rather than something that adds to it.

Arguably one could quote God's Commandment, "Thou Shall Not Kill," using this for their basis of conviction. They might also add that life is a gift from God and to take our own life is a crime against God. Many examples are provided in scripture of individuals suffering from fear, guilt, heartache, illness, pride, and hopelessness, but nowhere in God's Word does it indicate that suicide is an unforgivable sin. In fact, the Bible clearly defines that the only unforgivable sin is the denial of accepting Jesus Christ as our Lord and Savior.

Suicide certainly hurts the heart of God. We are all beautiful creations of God. Therefore, voluntarily giving up on life bestowed on us may look like an insult to God himself. The loved ones left behind there may be comfort in the fact that Jesus is a forgiving, loving, and caring being. I think in some small way, this will help Lindsey, bringing her a form of peace. It certainly comforts my sadness over the loss of a young teenager whose only crime was being in love.

So, what is love anyway? We know that we are commanded to love the Lord with all our heart, soul, and mind, but we're also commanded to love our neighbor like ourselves (Matthew 22:36-40).

Love defined in Merriam-Webster is multiple, and we know many have suffered, rejoiced, celebrated, killed, and died in the name of love. A word that is very powerful. A word that was never intended to be twisted, altered, diluted, or shared in a misconstrued manner. Yet as we view modern society, it has potentially become just that.

There are certainly many that are difficult to love within our life. The most important thing to remember is that denial can blind us to the truth. The truth is we are all sinners. We are all spiritually dead without the cross. When spirit became flesh and was placed upon a cross, crucified, died, and was resurrected, we all received a special gift, grace. We experience this gift by faith, not by works. Meaning that good deeds alone will not permit us to experience the fullness of grace. The realization that God's word is the timeless, applicable way of life will reward us with not only the fulfillment of grace but also the purpose and meaning of our own existence.

I would find that Jean Stevens had an unusual or unique interpretation of love. You will read about her very soon if you keep on reading. Jean would assign a definition to love that was unprecedented not only in our country but in the entire world.

A movie released in 1998 titled "Patch Adams" gives death a new meaning when the main character addresses a jury comprising of the best doctors and medical health professionals, saying, *"What's wrong with death, Sir? What are we so mortally afraid of? Why can't we treat death with a certain amount of humanity and dignity and decency and, God forbid, maybe even humor. Death is not the enemy, gentlemen. If we're going to fight a disease, let's fight one of the most terrible diseases of all, indifference. Now I've sat in your schools and heard people lecture on transference and professional distance. Transference is inevitable, Sir. Every human being has an impact on another. Why don't we want that in a patient-doctor relationship? I've listened to your teachings, and I believe they're wrong. A doctor's mission should be not just to prevent death but also to improve the quality of life. That's why when you treat a disease. You win. You lose. You treat a person. I guarantee you win no matter what the outcome."*

The true essence of the speech lies in knowing that death is not something to be afraid of, nor should it make you feel worthless or useless. Instead, it should make you stronger and far more resilient since the impact humans have on each other will continue to be so. We cannot detach ourselves from people and relationships, hoping it will take away all the sorrows that death brings. True happiness and contentment come with knowing that we are placed in each other's lives for a purpose – a purpose so simple but as meaningful as the air we breathe, the grass we run in, or the mountains we climb – we are here to help each other.

—— *Chapter 2* ——

NOBODY LEFT BEHIND

"There's an elderly woman over in Wyalusing who has her dead husband's corpse in her garage. I can't prove it, but there's talk about it," was far from the usual greeting the funeral director, Frankie Jones, would welcome me.

Frankie continued his story as we wheeled the stretcher into his building. "She and I had some contact recently. She called me about having her husband's grave dug up, something about too many rocks on top of him. So, I figured, why not? So, I sent over Anthony O'Connor with an excavator and Mike Haggar as a witness so they could freshen up the grave and remove the rocks."

"Odd, but it doesn't seem too strange," I replied as we positioned the stretcher next to the mortician's table.

"Well, it gets strange! She's waiting for them at the plot and orders them to expose the casket's top. Once that's done, she springs over, opens the casket, puts a beanie on his head, and replaces his shoes with booties!" I gave Frankie a surprised look and asked him what Anthony and Mike did as I carefully slid the decedent (deceased person) from the stretcher onto the mortician's table.

"Nearly shit themselves and ran into the woods. When she had finished her odd business, they approached her, and she asked them to wrap the casket in a blue tarp and reinter it with topsoil. She left soon after."

"Just left with no explanation?" I asked.

"None. And what makes me even more suspicious is that Anthony recently buried this woman's sister for her, and the grave is on this strange woman's property! While Anthony was working, he looked into the woman's garage, and there was a body-sized roll of tarp on the floor. All this happened over at Lime Hill if you want to look into it."

The decedent's sleeping countenance contrasted my puzzled expression as I wished Frankie a good day and returned the stretcher to my van.

That conversation introduced me to the most bizarre case I have dealt with as the Coroner of Bradford County, Pennsylvania. Throughout this chapter and the rest of the book, I want you to imagine yourself in my shoes and to contemplate what you might have done differently. In the State of Pennsylvania, the office of the County Coroner is elected. It's held by a regular citizen who has an investigative and medical background. I have confidence in my office as I've spent most of my life working in emergency medicine and death investigation, but I'm still a citizen doing my best as a human. There is no secret knowledge to what I do, just experience and methodology. So, ask yourself what you would have done if you had the correct answers to the situations this chapter puts me in.

A few days later, with Frank's story fresh in my mind, I was working with the State Police in the nearby town of Towanda on an unrelated case. I asked Tpr. Paul Fontelle and Cpl. Sam Finnerty what they thought of the woman and her supposed body collecting. Their first response was that this couldn't be an actual story, but after discussing it, we decided we'd be better off waiting for more information. It certainly did feel a little bizarre at first since none of us had thought we'd be having a case where a woman is obsessing over collecting dead bodies. But we also thought, why go barge into some older woman's house when there have been no complaints or reports? However, I left telling the officers that it was their problem anyway if something criminal was going on. I recall saying, "You'll be in the limelight on Lime Hill." With a grin. That statement would come back to bite me in a few months.

For the next several months, I was mystified by the idea of someone who wanted to keep a body in their house or garage. But I also believe that everyone has their reasons. Such an act could have a deeper meaning than the apparent. I work with bodies constantly, and the sooner they can be investigated, cleaned, and taken care of according to their wishes, the better. My first assumption is that this woman must have Alzheimer's Disease or some form of dementia. Maybe she thinks that her husband is still alive and that they shouldn't be buried. I know that death was strange to me when I was a child. Particularly troubling was watching my relatives when my uncle died in a construction accident when I was a young teen. The effects of loss on my mother and her side of the family were confusing. Death has always served as a reality check for everyone. People have their coping mechanisms, but some fail to cope altogether. So, it is here when a person gets motivated to do something strange and unacceptable.

I've seen many grieving relatives in my professional life, including all the stages of grief. At no point did anyone, regardless of religion, age, or education, genuinely believe their dead loved one was alive in this world as I showed them the body. Denial was one of the things that I saw as typical. Still, eventually, people do get acceptance of the death of their loved ones. Throughout my puzzling life, I responded to homicidal, suicidal, accidental, and natural deaths, writing death certificates and generally keeping as busy as a coroner in a rural county can be. Nothing I worked on during that time was wild enough to pull my imagination away from that woman collecting bodies.

Let's be honest about it. Would you, on your wildest day, consider co-residing with your dead loved one? I think it's safe to say, no, you wouldn't, nor would I. But I might have generalized my views a bit too much. Love or loneliness can drive people to be someone they aren't and do things they wouldn't typically do. So, when people say, "Everything is fair in love and war," some might actually mean it.

I'm reminded of February 1, 1988. I was 22, and Fred, who we all called "Freddie," was 20. Excluding my first true love I mentioned earlier, Freddy was my best friend at that time.

We were at my apartment after a long day of playing poker at the home of a mutual friend. It was the night of the 1988 Superbowl. The Skins beat the Broncos. After the game, Freddie and three other mutual friends came back to my apartment to continue poker.

Around 03:00, one of our friends needed a lift back to his house in a neighboring town. Freddie was spending the night with me, and we were leaving on a road trip the following day. Everyone agreed it was time to wrap the game up. Two of our friends resided uptown, so they walked home.

Freddie asked if I would ride with him to take our friend home. Being on a call with the ambulance and being tied to the phone, I really couldn't leave. I declined, then said, "Wear your seat belt." Freddie had one of those Ford Escort GTs that were very fast. He hated to wear his seat belt. He would always put it behind him and then buckle it in. I often told him how this would cost him his life one day, but Freddie didn't heed it at all.

I told Freddie, "You should be back in 25 minutes," as they were leaving. It was a 10-minute ride down, another ten back, with 5 minutes to spare. He smirked and asked, "Are you sure you don't want to ride down?"

I knew I wouldn't be seeing him alive again when he left. Many would call me crazy, but I know I felt it, and my intuitions were never wrong. I went out to the kitchen and boiled water for a cup of coffee. Once done, I went into the living room and turned-on HBO to watch my favorite on-air documentary

I sat there and gazed at the clock on my wall; it was now 20 minutes since Freddie had left. I stood up and started to pace. Call me crazy, but I could feel what was about to happen. I started palpitating, and my palms got sweaty. It had now been 25 minutes since they left.

Suddenly, the emergency telephone line rang. I went in and picked up the receiver to carefully listen to what the caller was stating. I heard an older woman say, there's been an accident in front of my house, and the young blonde hair boy is lying in the road.

I held on to the receiver, knowing in my heart, this was Freddie, and he was dead. The memories I made with him flashed before my eyes as I began to lose my conscience. It felt like a bad dream, and I was hoping Freddie would wake me up from it. I somberly walked across the street to the ambulance garage to meet my driver. My driver that night just so happened to live next door to the station, kitty-corner.

He rapidly met me at the station. I was emotionally upset, which led Bob to ask me what was wrong. I informed him I knew who this was. Bob stated you don't know; maybe he is stuck in line at the scene. I said, "No, I know it's Freddie." I had never been that sure in my life before.

We arrived on the scene, and I saw Freddie's vehicle on the side of the southbound lane facing south. I could see his vehicle had rolled. I immediately went up to it. Inside, I noted the seatbelt buckled in, and sadly, he had it behind him! I also noted one of his white sneakers inside the vehicle, but no Freddie. Upon seeing the situation, my heart skipped a beat. After that, I couldn't think of anything else but constantly question myself about where Freddie was.

I turned and looked across the road where a gathering of fire personnel stood. I started to walk over when I noticed the second sneaker in the roadway. As I walked closer, a friend of mine with the fire service approached me, stating, "Tom, you don't want to go up there."

I pushed my way through until I was in front of one of the worse sights I had seen. In front of me was Freddie. He lay on the roadway face up with no shoes. His eyes were wide open, looking at me. It was apparent that he had been struck and drug up the road from another vehicle that was not on the scene.

The next thing I know, I wake up the following morning in the hospital. I had gone into shock. It was one of the worst moments of my life, and I wish I could undo it. My mother was at the bedside. Finally, I was discharged and sent on my way.

When I first arrived at my apartment, it was strange. I opened the door and gazed into the kitchen, where we all had been just the other night. The table still was as we left it, cards and all. The denim jacket Freddie had left next to my own was on the living room chair. It was as if he knew he wasn't coming back. I still have his jacket hanging in my closet with my clothes. It felt unreal, as though something was clenching my throat.

This event is still fresh on my mind. It changed me forever. Even though my love for Freddie ran deep, I couldn't imagine keeping his remains with me in my apartment. He was gone, and there was no way he was coming back. Even the remains wouldn't do justice to his live presence

Even in the wildest days, the thought of having the remains of a deceased loved one being anywhere other than a grave or in an urn on a mantle was just not acceptable, ethical, or even logical. So, if the Jean Stevens story is true, I can't fathom why.

The question of why is always perplexing and periodically remains a mystery. Why are some attracted to the same sex while others are attracted to the opposite? Why do some find enjoyment in music while others are completely unaffected by it? Many whys go unanswered, although many theories exist. But to me, the question of why is fundamental. It is the only way humans can know the science and the reasoning behind everything unknown to humankind.

The average human adult brain weighs between 1,300 to 1,400 grams or 3 pounds. Although relatively small compared to the average adult torso, the brain is instrumental in our everyday decisions.

Simply put, the frontal lobe and limbic cortex are associated with both problem-solving and emotional regulation. Likewise, the parietal cortex and amygdala are linked to both social and sexual behavior. However, it is the neurons that transmit and carry information and allow different parts of the brain to communicate with the parts of our bodies.

You may or may not find this exciting, but more importantly, this explains why people do what they do. For example, why does a serial killer kill? Why does an individual make a conscious decision to kill a child? Why does an individual choose to drive their car head-on into a tree versus hanging or gunshot when committing suicide?

It would be exhilarating to point to a specific area of the brain and say, here's the answer but reality reflects otherwise. How nice would it be if it were possible. Think of the potential. A simple MRI would predict serial murder, sexuality, and suicidal intent. It would be an asset to the judiciary and the authorities and help minimize crimes and deviancies.

On March 15, 2019, Psychology Today published "Understanding What Drives a Serial Killer." The article quotes the FBI report "Serial Killers," released in 2005. A serial killer selects their victims based upon "Availability, vulnerability, and desirability." The FBI continues that likely motives are:

1. Anger is a powerful motivation in which the offender displays rage or hostility towards a certain population subgroup, such as the homeless or society.

2. Criminal enterprise is a motivation in which the offender benefits in status or monetary reward by committing mur-

der that is drug, gang, or organized crime-related. For example, murder may be perpetrated by a drug gang to eliminate its competition.

3. Financial gain is a motivation in which the offender benefits monetarily from drugs, gangs, or organized crime-related killing. Examples of these crimes are comfort/gain killings, robbery-homicide, or multiple killings involving insurance or welfare fraud.

4. Ideology is a motivation where you murder to further the goals and ideas of a specific individual or group. Examples of these include terrorist groups or individual(s) who attack a specific racial, gender or ethnic group out of sheer hatred for the group.

5. Power/thrill is a motivation in which the offender feels empowered and exhilarated when they kill their victims. The act of killing is an end in itself.

6. Psychosis is a rare situation in which the offender has a severe mental illness and is killing specifically because of that illness. The condition may include auditory or visual hallucinations, paranoia, grandiose or bizarre delusions. For example, Leon Hutchinson was a long-term mental health patient who suffered from a paranoid delusion. He used a four-inch knife to fatally and repeatedly stab his flat mate, Damilola 'Danny' Wilson. He was repeatedly stabbed in the face and neck, causing severe and massive blood loss.

7. Sexual-based motivation is driven by the offender's sexual needs or desires. There may or may not be evidence of sexual contact present at the crime scene.

With or without understood motive, serial killers are drawn to commit murder. They do it because they want to and need to. Considering they are the least understood, thankfully, serial killings are the rarest form of homicide. But a serial killer on the loose is the worst purge humanity has ever witnessed. It almost feels like a wild dog unleashed.

The most common type of homicide is single murder. We can potentially allocate some or all of the FBI-identified motives for serial murder to individuals who commit a single act of homicide. However, the element of thrill and sexual gratification is seldom a motive for a single homicide. Of course, there are always exceptions to every rule.

A few years back, I had a case that involved a nearly 2-year-old female. The perpetrator was a white male in his mid-twenties. He was the boyfriend of the female victim's mother. It was not unusual for the perpetrator to be left alone with the victim throughout the day. The mother was gainfully employed and ran multiple errands daily. The perpetrator was not employed and had a free ride with this recently divorced white female. The mother was moderately obese and expressed low self-esteem. On the day of the murder, the mother was at her place of employment.

While at work, she received a call from the perpetrator. The call was unprecedented, informing her that the victim, named Lydia, was ill and now lying in her makeshift playpen sleeping. This was very unusual and concerning, so the mother immediately left work and returned home. Upon arriving home, the mother discovered her daughter Lydia's lifeless body laying within her playpen. She immediately contacted 911, which began a trail of events, including the arrival of my office.

Upon the arrival of PSP and my office, Lydia was discovered in the playpen. She presented in underwear only with a bath towel near her. Upon a quick superficial exam, a small abrasion was noted on the bridge of the nose and a small abrasion to the left orbital area. The injuries were fresh, with no sign of initial or aged healing. This was of great concern. A rectal temperature revealed a slightly hypothermic result of 95.8, but this was of no concern because the postmortem interval was no more than 2 hours. We must also keep in mind that the smaller body mass of a child will likely cool much quicker than the average-sized adult.

An initial interview of the mother was conducted to gather any information on both Lydia and the male perpetrator. Lydia was a healthy and perfectly developing child. Unfortunately, the natural father and mother had divorced, with the husband leaving her. My heart went out to the poor child who still had a long journey ahead but unfortunately met death before seeing what life had to offer her.

The mother had met the perpetrator a few months earlier online. She described the perpetrator as very helpful. She went on to state that the perpetrator does not work but watches Lydia so she can work and support the family. She went on to state that the relationship between her and the perpetrator was good.

When asked to describe the relationship between the perpetrator and Lydia, she stated they were very close. Lydia would even snuggle with him while watching television. Lydia eventually grew fond of him and wanted him to be with her at all times. The latter suggests one of the main trick's perpetrators pull – getting close to the victim.

The perpetrator was a thin, tattooed, and bearded male. His initial presentation was that of an arrogant and defensive man. His testimony to the chain of events looked rehearsed. Further, he presented himself in a way of only trying to help Lydia. Such testimonies suggest that the perpetrator is trying to act naive and avoids foul play accusations.

When asked about what happened that afternoon, he stated Lydia was crying and running a fever. He went on to say that he placed the victim in a cold bath in an attempt to reduce the proposed fever. When specifically asked what happened while Lydia was in the tub, the perpetrator indicated that Lydia would not sit still and ultimately fell forward, striking her head and nose on the bathtub spout. Now we have him locked into a statement. His initial statement is documented regardless of where he navigates his story moving forward. His story never altered from his initial statement throughout his interview.

A couple of days later, we would learn that the perpetrator had moved out of the mother's home. He was now residing with his father in a different county. We would also learn that the perpetrator had visited a friend's home. While at the friend's house, he had exposed himself to a 14-year-old male in an attempt to have sex with this child. Now we know we are dealing with a child predator. When you think about sexual offenses, the motivation may stem from the self-regulatory problems and problematic behavior of the perpetrators.

Initially, DNA samples and certain items had been submitted to the crime lab. Upon receipt of the DNA results for our case, it was determined that the bath towel discovered within the playpen had semen from the perpetrator. Also revealed was trace semen discovered on Lydia's face that matched the perpetrator's DNA.

Upon completing the investigation, the perpetrator confessed to placing the victim in the bathtub and masturbating upon her. When the victim attempted to move before he finished, the perpetrator slammed her head on the tub spout. Then, in an attempt to cover his crime, he placed Lydia in the playpen. As she lay crying, he placed the semen-stained towel across her face, suffocating Lydia.

The perpetrator is a manipulative, controlling, and deviant predator who would stop at nothing to cover his actions and silence his victim. Many may characterize him as an opportunist. But we believed he was a pedophile who escalated to murder to go unnoticed—a true example of evil. As his intention was unveiled, we got to know that he would have gone to any lengths to sexually gratify himself, even if it took him murdering someone innocent or doing something he hadn't thought of initially.

As another example, I had a case that would illustrate a different type of motive. This case involved a middle-aged woman who I shall leave nameless. However, for this example, we shall give her the name "The one who got away."

This case started when I was contacted to go to a local emergency department. The victim was a three-month-old infant. The infant presented hypothermic with well-developed rigor. Consequently, we immediately learned that the death or postmortem interval window period is potentially 2-6 hours. This differs with adults; however, rigor will set in quicker with an infant of 3 months with a very small body mass.

Simply put, we know there was a delay in contacting 911 for the n an unknown reason. Usually, when there is a delay in contacting the police, the crime may have been done by the person who had made the call to the authorities or took time to cover up traces that could endanger the murderer.

The preliminary examination in the emergency department came up short for anomalies, except for the left forehead, where we discovered a discoloration and indentation resembling an imprint of a piece of jewelry.

Medical records were reviewed, revealing no concerns. There were no underlying medical explanations. This was a healthy, well-developed 3-month-old.

This office performed preliminary radiographic studies to rule out any internal trauma. X-rays revealed no underlying trauma such as age or acute fractures. Lungs were filled with fluid commonly referred to as pulmonary edema. Generically we could say they were heavy and wet. This can be the result of a chronic disease or an acute event. In this case, we knew that no medical conditions could explain this finding. Consequently, this was more than likely a sharp end to life. It is true how medical science can sometimes fail to answer the questions of need and may leave dead ends.

The mother of this infant is not at the emergency department, which is concerning. Why wouldn't a mother be with her child at the hospital? Instead, the mother was at her residence, where we needed to go to process the scene and interview her.

The mother is an obese female weighing an estimated 350 pounds. She presents with a standoff nature and is snarky with her responses. Immediately noted on her left ring finger is a piece of jewelry with a design that perfectly matches the indentation discovered on the infant's forehead. She was not happy that we were present at her doorstep. Her reaction was contrary to what we had expected. A mother should be concerned and under immense stress when the police report her about her infant, but here the mother seemed unhinged and carefree.

It was explained that we would be examining her residence for anything that would help explain her child's death. She provides verbal consent. This was an apartment of good size. Within it was a large master bedroom. Upon examining the bedroom, it was noted that there was a crib in the room. Next, the bed was examined where the mother slept. There were two large pillows with sheets and a comforter. All items were closely examined as we searched for bodily fluids, including vomit, clear or blood-tinged fluid, as well as blood. The bedding superficially appeared to be unremarkable. The mattress was examined next to evaluate how firm it was or if it would fold in the middle with the mother's weight on it. From the EMS providers who transported, we came to know that the mother had offered a statement indicating that she was co-sleeping with the infant. Upon completing the initial examination of the apartment, it was time to interview the mother.

With any child death, getting a statement within the first 24 hours is critical. The late it gets, the far you get from the offender. The next critical item to gather in any death is a timeline. The timeline can vary in length based on the investigated incident, window of death, and any significant findings before death.

The mother sticks to her initial story presented to EMS. She states that she was co-sleeping with the infant and awoke to find her not breathing. It is common for our office to use a life-sized doll for the individual to show us precisely the positioning of not only themselves but also the victim.

When asked about the infant's head's indentation, she explained that maybe her hand was resting on the infant's head as they slept. This could potentially explain these findings, but the indentation was rather deep and detailed for the normal resting hand. It finally started to feel like we were getting to know something of substance.

But the mother would not deviate from her account of the events. Instead, she insisted that they were co-sleeping, and while doing so, she must have rolled onto the victim.

Now that mom was locked into a statement, we would wait for the autopsy examination to see any hidden findings. Upon conclusion of the autopsy, we would learn that no significant findings could contradict the mother's statement.

Continuing with the investigation over the next week, we would discover that the mother had lost her second child. Digging deeper, we would discover that the first infant also died while co-sleeping with the mother. Now we have a problem.

While speaking with the pediatrician who cared for both infants, he explained that he instructed the mother not to co-sleep with any additional children due to her size after the first death. This was excellent information to have, but we hoped that it was documented. However, to our surprise, medical records revealed that it was documented at the time.

Having acquired this new information and a cause of death of Sudden Unexplained Infant Death While Co-Sleeping with an Adult would turn the manner from accidental to homicide. We would base this on because this is the second child that has died. The mother had been medically instructed not to ever co-sleep with a child.

The state police and our office were in agreement that the manner should be a homicide. However, we can only establish the cause and manner of death. It is not within our scope of practice to take an individual to trial.

Consequently, this woman was never formally charged with homicide and still walks the streets today. In addition, the final death certificate was worded so that it will be forever red-flagged with the state. Hopefully, this will prevent any other children from dying while co-sleeping with their mothers.

My concern with the death of this infant was not just the obvious did the mother suffer from Munchausen syndrome by proxy, or had she discovered a way to commit homicide by hiding behind the façade of co-sleeping?

The motives were unclear in both of these cases. Motives are not always guaranteed, and some would say ignore the motive initially and focus on the individual. This makes perfect sense to me. After all, the presence of a motive doesn't mean that an individual would commit an act. Likewise, the lack of motive doesn't mean someone would not commit an act, but many other times, it is the motives that may give a head start to any act of violence and thus shouldn't be ignored by the authorities. After all, an innocent person is very likely to suffer if motives are not considered.

— *Chapter 3* —

THE MISSION
BELL RINGS

On June 15, 2010, I finally got a call. Area Agency on Aging Supervisor Kathleen Most informed me that one of their Agency caseworkers was alerted that an elderly lady had the body of her deceased twin sister in her house. The caseworker had seen the body during a follow-up visit. I asked Kathleen if this was in Lime Hill, Wyalusing. The answer was "Yes." I immediately arranged for a meeting with the county district attorney and state police to occur the next day. Though this situation was unique, working together like this is not. A significant part of my office is coordinating activities related to death investigation and bringing relevant parties together. The cohesion of all the relevant parties is of immense significance for solving any case. Imagine having scattered shreds of evidence. It sure would make solving cases a strenuous job for all.

The next day, District Attorney Lyle Smith, Kathleen Most, Marlene Hicks (the caseworker who witnessed the body), and Cpl were assembled at the barracks of Sam Finnerty. The details of the situation were made clear to all at the meeting. Jean Lucille Stevens, 91, had the remains of her twin sister in her house. The potential laws being violated were:

Title 18 Section 5510 "Abuse of a Corpse," a second-degree misdemeanor, is defined as when someone treats a corpse in a way that he knows would outrage ordinary family sensibilities.

Title 28 Health and Safety, Section 1.25 Disinterment of Dead Human Bodies, Subsection Exhumation and Exposure. "The remains of any dead body shall not be exhumed and exposed to view without an order from a court of competent jurisdiction." Exhumation is controversial even if the intent is usually to rebury, displaced remains elsewhere. Most societies and cultures that embrace burial as a means of bodily disposal exhibit an entrenched reluctance to disturb the dead's earthly repose for two reasons. The first concerns public health concerns around the potential disease transmission from decaying corpses. Secondly, and more fundamentally, exhumation offends the basic moral premise of allowing the dead to 'rest in peace' and is generally regarded as a forbidden or sinful act. As a result, exhumation in England and Wales is subject to strict legal controls.

So right there, you have legal concerns. She is breaking the law if there is a body in Jean Stevens's house. Also of concern is the health and wellness of Jean herself. We did not want to rattle her by barging in and strong-arming any remains out of her possession. Diplomacy would be the best route especially considering our suspicions that she was crazy or demented. We had no intention of triggering anything Jean was sensitive to or doing anything that would put her in peril. Because of this, we had Marlene lead the way as Jean already knew her. We also called for an ambulance to be on hand if Jean became agitated and needed medical assistance.

After obtaining a warrant for the search of Jean's house and premises, we set out.

During the 25- minute drive from Towanda to Lime Hill, I wondered about the news media's interest in the case. I've never been overly excited about being swarmed by the media. Honestly, I'd instead be working. However, there was also no denying that Jean's case would make for excellent media material. The media has always had a thirst for controversial yet eye-gripping news.

In fact, the only similar scenario I'm personally aware of occurred in 1933 by the late Dr. Carl Tanzler, sometimes called Count Carl von Cosel (February 8, 1877 – July 3, 1952). Almost two years after her death, Tanzler removed his true love and patient's body from its tomb and lived with the corpse at his home for seven years (source: Wikipedia).

I also speculated about what we might find in the house. Would there be bodies propped up in chairs? Would we discover her eating lunch next to a stale corpse? I was determined to follow the law here and confiscate any human remains for storage in my refrigerated morgue. What to do about Jean herself was the mystery. We were in a fix and had yet to strategize dealing with her.

Jean's house was not hidden from the road, but it was nearly 300 meters from the nearest neighbor and surrounded by trees. The structure seemed sound though it was in great need of a new coat of paint. So far, this seemed pretty typical for an older adult's house in rural PA. Why wouldn't it be? The permanence of loneliness and inactivity wouldn't motivate anyone to renovate their house. After all, it is just the old lady and her thoughts living in the house. The time of our arrival was 14:58, June 15th, 2010.

FIG. 1 JEAN L. STEVENS RESIDENCE LOCATED IN WYALUSING TOWNSHIP.
PHOTO BY THOMAS M. CARMAN

We approached the front door and braced ourselves for whatever awaited us on the other side. But honestly speaking, I was a bit excited to know what we were to welcome. Our knock was greeted with a "Come in!" from inside. Upon entering, we were greeted by a smiling older woman sitting at the dining room table. The first things I noticed were that the house was clean, no decedents were seated at the table, and the house smelled strongly of mothballs. This immediately took me back in time. I had smelled this same smell as a kid in my grandmother's upstairs. The aroma of mothballs was a sad reminder of days past. I vividly remember that the mothballs were used to keep the mice and moths away from the clothing. At least, this is what I was told whenever I asked. Honestly, I wouldn't say I liked this odor at all. However, it was nostalgic to know that Jean's house reflected my grandmother's and had that signature geriatric touch.

The older woman was Jean, and she was wearing a light blue knit shirt, a dark blue cloth skirt, and sneakers, and she had her hair up in a bun. She was not messy or unhealthy looking. She seemed very much together for a 91-year-old woman that was allegedly crazy. As we began noticing her little details, we grew confident that Jean was everything but not a mentally challenged person.

One odd thing noted at the table was a setting of a plate, platter, tea cup, and spoon were all laid out for a second person who was not at the table. To me, it felt like she was awaiting someone to join her.

Fig. 2 Front door entrance into the kitchen.
Photo by Thomas M. Carman

After everyone had arrived inside, Cpl Finnerty produced his search warrant and politely asked Jean if she had any questions. She declined to ask any and answered all of Finnerty's inquiries with a smile. Jean was aware of why we were interested and concerned, but she didn't seem phased at all. It seemed like she had rehearsed the entire situation in her mind.

"Mrs. Stevens, I understand you have your twin sister, June, in the house. Is this true? Have you?" asked Finnerty.

"Yes," she replied.

Then, just as I was thinking to myself, "That was easy," Jean spoke again, "Would you like to meet her?" Without missing a beat, Finnerty replied, "Why yes. I would."

Jean sprung up from her seat as though she was 30 years younger and led us through her house as though it was a tour. Quaint furnishings littered with relics of her nearly century-long life filled the house, and there seemed to be an abundance of television sets throughout the house.

FIG. 3 LIVING ROOM. PHOTO BY THOMAS M. CARMAN

We finally arrived at a side room she called the spare bedroom. This room was a little more in line with what you'd expect a room holding a stolen body to look like.

This room was once painted with light blue walls and had white wainscoting (decorative paneling) at the base of the walls. The paint was peeling badly, and a lot of plaster had fallen from the walls. The rafters were visible in much of the room. Being a coroner doesn't just involve investigating bodies. The body's environment can be rather informative and revealing, but here the atmosphere seemed a bit puzzling.

FIG. 4 SPARE BEDROOM. PHOTO BY THOMAS M. CARMAN

After only a little more than 15 minutes in Jean's house, we were introduced to her dead twin. June was found supine (lying on her back) wrapped in layers of blankets. Her face was not completely covered, and on a dresser next to her body was an armada of powders, ointments, and a bottle of perfume. June's glasses were in place, and her golden-gray hair was also in good condition. Her skin was hardened like plastic, and her eyes were just open slits. There was a fake white flower tucked into her hair. The smell of mothballs and perfume was strong. I was although a coroner and had seen a lot of dreadful cases, but this one was weirdly saddening

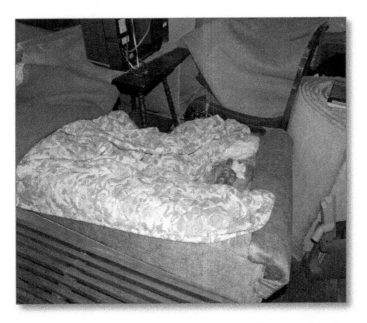

Fig 5. June's remains on the sofa. Photo by Thomas M. Carman

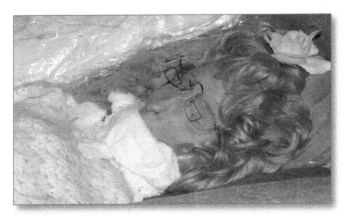

Fig. 6 June's remains up close. Photo by Thomas M. Carman

At this point, it was just the officers in the room with Jean, and except for Jean, we all had dumbfounded looks on our faces. This situation was made even more bizarre by Jean's casual nature about it. She seemed too nonchalant for someone who has a dead body stored in her house.

Jean had been taking cosmetic care of her twin as though she was a very morbid doll. She was also doing her best to cover up the smells of an embalmed body with perfume and lotions. Yes, I said an embalmed body. June had initially been embalmed before being buried.

Now mind you, The EPA has classified formaldehyde as a probable human carcinogen. Cancer Institute researchers have concluded that based on studies in people and lab research, exposure to formaldehyde may cause Leukemia, particularly Myeloid Leukemia in humans (source-www.cancer.org). I was even more confused about Jean's mental state now. Why was she different around the deceased than everyone else? Could it be possible that she was hiding something from us?

After taking it all in, Cpl. Finnerty popped the question about Jean's husband. "Are there other bodies here?"

"Yes, Jimmy is in the garage," proclaimed Jean. "But first, I need to get the garage door opener." But, again, Jean was very casual. It was as though we were visiting acquaintances interested in meeting her 'housemates.' In more ways than one, this situation is anything than grave to her.

I placed my hand on Tpr. Fontenelle's shoulder and said, "Shall we?" With a grin on my face. But, please understand, this grin was out of pure disbelief and wondering what I would do with these bodies. After all, this was a first for me. Can you imagine, though? Years of being a coroner and having to miss a likewise peculiarity in a case.

Fig 7 The garage. Photo by Thomas M. Carman

The garage was a vinyl-sided freestanding building. It was the same one that held the bundle of tarp Anthony Salada saw.

The garage, as seen in Figure 7, was cluttered. The station wagon appeared to have not been used for some time. To the left of the wagon was a sofa. Jean indicates that this is where her late husband, James "Jimmy" Mark Stevens, rests. We've been at her house for less than 30 minutes, and we've found two bodies. "What more does this woman have in store?" I silently wondered. Could she be unaware of her actions or perhaps is aware, but is in denial of her behavior and the reasoning behind her actions.

We decided to call in a forensics team before unwrapping Jimmy. The role of a PA State Police Forensic Unit is to document the scene using photography and to collect items of evidential value.

Within a couple of hours, Tpr. Tim Friedman arrived on the scene to document everything. He exclaimed to me that he'd never seen anything like this as he worked his way through the house taking photos. I agreed.

He took photos in series as we cautiously unwrapped June to expose her as she is in Figure 6. It turns out she was dressed in a red nightgown. A foolish thought, but it seemed like we were dealing with a case involving the occult. After photo documentation, I carefully placed June into a body bag and then moved her to my vehicle for further detailed examination at my morgue.

Next up was Jimmy's bundle. He was covered with a blue tarp (possibly the same one the grave diggers placed around his casket), and below that, newspapers dating back to October 14, 2001.

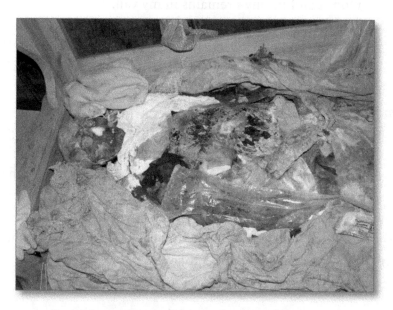

FIG. 8 JAMES "JIMMY" MARK STEVENS ON A SOFA.
PHOTO BY THOMAS M. CARMAN

Jimmy was not in as good shape as June. I thought this might explain his positioning in the garage while June got the VIP treatment in the house. Now, at that point, I did not know if the two decedents were, in fact, June and Jimmy, and to proceed with this investigation, I would need to take them back to my morgue for my detailed examination. Surprisingly Jean did not become angry with us when we left with her relative's bodies. She seemed comfortable with them being taken as though they were just going for a trip in my van. This was when some understanding of her condition began to make itself known to me. She hated the thought of traditional burial first and foremost. Her physical proximity to them did not matter as much as that. It was also obvious she was rational enough to understand that she could be in legal trouble if she opposed the authorities. I believed her to be sane and her actions to have meaning even if everyone else held her accountable. Without much trouble, I left the scene at Lime Hill with June's and Jimmy's remains in my van.

My office and morgue are located in Troy, PA, about a 45-minute drive from Lime Hill. The decedents were both relatively light. Both were dry, previously embalmed bodies. This means they didn't have much water weight. Jimmy barely weighed 27Kg (60lb), and June even less than Jimmy.

Moving the deceased can often be a significant undertaking, especially in the case of obese decedents, and the ease of working with embalmed bodies is not lost on me. When I arrived at my office, I moved them to the cooler, essentially a smaller and cleaner version of a walk-in fridge at a restaurant. It was now 21:35 when I had everything done, so I called it a night. The day felt like a thriller movie, except that we reached no climax today.

Chapter 4

IT HAS TO BE 5 O'CLOCK SOMEWHERE

At this point in my life, a good stiff drink always took away the stress of the job. Music and vodka worked miraculously to make the sights, sounds, and stress disappear, or so I thought. Floating on a raft inside a tall bottle of Grey Goose, looking out through the frosted bottle brought an ephemeral sense of peace in those days. However, the following mornings always sucked. I felt like a dry sponge that had been tossed on the sink board. But I do believe that despite everything, the show must go on!

I try to exclude myself, considering that I was a malefactor, although I reluctantly admit that alcohol was a big part of my life. The feeling of the first sip of the booze kicking in gave me the ultimate pleasure and joy. I remember enjoying my first cold beer at 12 when my uncle Felix threw a kegger picnic and handed me a cold one. Hell, in the town I grew up in, weekend campfires and parties were the norms. You were viewed as abnormal if you didn't party like a party animal. But deep down, I knew I would eventually have to pay the price by finally abstaining from it. And this is precisely what has happened since, at least for the past four years.

June 16, 2010, started bright and early at 08:00. It was investigation time. Here is my method for handling a usual case broken down into six parts to give you a sense of a death investigation. These methods represent victimology, psychological autopsy, and anatomical autopsy:

Who is the decedent? Is there a past medical history of any kind? Any and all medical history helps. Where has the decedent lived throughout their life? This is important for tracking down relatives, friends, medical documents, and so much more.

What was the decedent's motivation/outlook on life? Have they abused drugs? Have they done time in prison? Have they ever attempted suicide or mentioned being suicidal? Learning these facts can help guide me toward an answer. A suicide becomes less suspicious if a decedent was abusing alcohol and not taking their antidepressant medication as prescribed.

Investigation of the facts. This involves family, friends, associates, and eyewitness testimony. They can tell me where they found the body, what the scene was like, and other salient information. The more information, the better I can compare it to what others say, and it can also be compared against physical evidence. Also, such pieces of facts usually contribute to the complete success of an investigation as well.

External examination of the body. This entire body examination includes recording hair color and length, body weight and size (not height!), scars, tattoos, and piercings. It's also a search for injuries and tissue norms or abnormalities. Again, the minutest of details will be recorded and preserved here.

Forensic autopsy. I am a coroner, not a medical examiner, so I work with forensic pathologists in a nearby city. I witnessed the autopsy and recorded the findings, ultimately certifying the cause and manner of death on the death certificate. The abdominal cavity is opened during a complete autopsy, and organs are inspected, weighed, and dissected. The brain is removed and inspected if needed. Finally, the body gains a second life in the eyes of the pathologist. The pathologist is then able to probe deeply into the underlying facts. They can see what damage has occurred, and in turn, I can find how that damage may have been caused at the scene of the death.

Meeting the needs of the surviving family. This is the final and most crucial element in most of my work. I am responsible for storing and handling the body of their loved ones. It's an obligation and an act of caring during what might be the worst time in their lives. The funeral home handles everything related to final disposal, and by working closely with the chosen funeral home, I ensure less stress for the family involved. The grieving family has already been through a lot, so I cut them some slack by allowing them to relax.

Interestingly enough, I can apply all of these typical steps to dealing with Jean's case. Because this death involved two bodies of likely identity, I started with part 3, investigating the facts and looking for witnesses of Jean's behavior.

Later, I called up DiGiorno Funeral Home and inquired about the death of June E. Stevens and her burial situation. David DiGiorno provided some critical facts, such as the Connecticut city June died in and the time of death. Jean initially said that she didn't want to bury June at all, but David informed her that in PA, the deceased needed to either be buried, cremated, or placed in a crypt. This was the norm, but since we know Jean, the case's protagonist, always had an otherwise opinion and ways. At first, she was adamant about this but relented having June buried under topsoil on her property. On October 12, 2009, this burial occurred less than a year before we discovered June on the sofa.

At this point, you might have noticed Jean's preference for topsoil. First, she complained about Jimmy having too many rocks on him and requested that he be covered only with loose soil. Now you have Jean asking for topsoil over her sister. Part of this could be her mindset of a burial, but more likely, she wants to dig up her loved ones quickly. This is a good sign that the remains are, in fact, her relatives and not some third party.

David went on to tell me that a few days after the legal burial on Jean's property, he stopped by to check on her and saw her carrying three large, clean buckets while wearing hip boots. The most suspicious bit was a blue tarp covering the grave. Upon questioning Dave, Jean informed him there was too much water near June's grave, so she was draining it. Dave was disturbed by this whole situation and gave a call to Jean's neighbors (who were friends with her also) and told them to keep an eye on her. It was justified for Dave to be astonished since we all considered Jean capable of pulling dangerous acts like she had been doing. Before I left David, I asked him if he thought Jean had Alzheimer's Disease. David's response was, "She knows exactly what she is doing and has planned this from the beginning." Honestly, I was hoping he would say otherwise, but this did line up with the evidence and had causally been proven right.

Jean had been taken to see a doctor by an Area Agency on Aging representative because of her extreme interest in the grave. The doctor thoroughly examined her. As a result, she was declared fully competent and not a mentally deranged human.

At mid-morning on June 16, 2010, I called Salada Excavating and scheduled Anthony Salada to help me exhume the graves of Jimmy and June. Even if there might not be a body, digging up a grave is still an exhumation and requires a court order in the State of Pennsylvania.

As I walked out of the courthouse holding this document, I noticed the weather was turning bad. It was like a B-list horror movie. The storm came with a sepia hint to the silver-black sky, as if it already knew the winds and rain it wrought would echo for eternity. Lightning seemed to crack the sky, sending heaven's light through the storms. Dark clouds and rain mists appeared in the distance as I proceeded to disturb the graves of the dead. Fortunately, by the time I met up with Anthony on Lime Hill, the sun was back out, and it was great weather for digging.

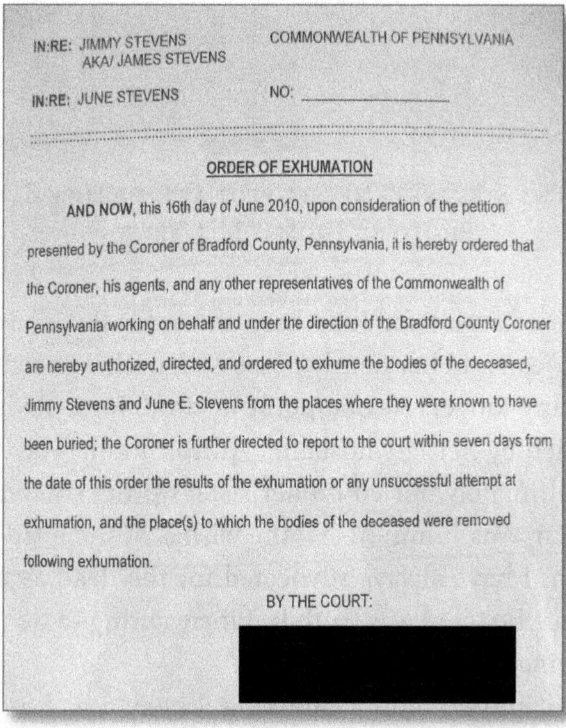

FIG. 9 ORDER OF EXHUMATION. PHOTO BY THOMAS M. CARMAN

The Lime Hill Cemetery was about 1 mile from Jean's house, and there were three grave plots for the Stevens family. First, James "Jimmy" Mark Stevens was off to one side on his own, then a double plot next to him was marked for Allison "Kemp" Stevens (June's husband) and June "Matson" Stevens. Note that the twin sisters June and Jean did, in fact, marry the brothers, Jimmy and Kemp, neither of which could have children. This is a strange story, isn't it?

FIG. 10 JUNE STEVENS CEMETERY PLOT AT LIME HILL CEMETERY.
PHOTO BY THOMAS M. CARMAN

The presence of a plot for June here was odd. But considering the oddities that Jean and her family possessed, nothing seemed unusual to our eyes any longer. At one point in time, June obviously wanted to be buried by her late husband, Allison Kemp Stevens. However, she was ultimately buried on her sister's property. Was she in on Jean's plan? Or Was Jimmy? Now the wishes of the dead are coming into question. I have always advocated for the dead as much as the living, and maybe there was truth in June wanting to be close to Jean even after dying.

Before I could do more wondering, I knew I had to ensure Jimmy was not actually buried beneath me. However, it was indeed an actual possibility since we were coming across graves minute by minute. Shortly, Anthony and I realized that he was buried in a natural wood casket, meaning that by now, we would probably just find rotten wood and loose bones if he was in there.

Anthony excavated the grave quickly, and we only found wood remnants. The sifting through it revealed no skeletal remains but did reveal broken pieces of headstones used to fill the body's place. Indeed, Jimmy had been snatched from his grave.

We moved ourselves and the excavator over to Jean's house. Jean was waiting and posed the question. Is this really necessary? I told her we had to verify the remains were, in fact, who she said they were.

June's grave was in a bit of field separated from the backyard by a tree-lined path. It was a very serene and beautiful location. To me, this would have been a more suitable eulogy to the deceased than a memorial.

As we were setting up, Tpr. Ted Gorski arrived to film the exhumation for the sake of evidence. We found the ground around the grave very wet due to a nearby spring, and the grave itself was visible because of Jean's disturbance of the soil months earlier. Nevertheless, the digging proceeded without difficulty.

FIG. 11 JUNE BURIAL SITE. PHOTO BY THOMAS M. CARMAN

The remains of a simple casket were discovered in the clay-like soil. I pondered over the fact that it was uncanny of Jean to choose a cheap coffin. However, she didn't intend to keep her sister in it for very long. But, as suspected, there wasn't anyone in that casket. This meant that, yes, the two bodies found were likely who Jean said they were. So, I was determined to verify the bodies themselves did come from those graves, which meant it was time for medical scrutiny.

As we left Jean's backyard, our search party noticed a news van from a local TV station parked on the side of the road. But this was something I was getting used to. I had already received some phone calls and visits from local journalists, but soon after, I began getting calls from national news, such as The Associated Press and The Wall Street Journal. The term "Mummies" quickly caught on in headlines.

The public interest in the story drove us to host a press conference in Towanda. I, along with the district attorney Barrett, Cpl. Ogden and Lt. Krawetz acted as a panel to give information and answer questions. Most of their questions were centered around Jean's well-being. Why did she do this, and what was going to happen to her were the questions that the panel was bombarded with. However, I answered to the best of my ability, but I still couldn't explain why Jean acted the way she did. It was more bothersome to me than it was for reporters. I could not even try postulating while the press had the luxury of simply speculating and calling it a day.

My mind is designed to work on what, how, and why. There had to be a reason Jean made the decisions she had made. She appears to be sane, so I knew the only way to find the answers was to invest a lot of time in her and understand her thought process.

CHERYL R. CLARKE/Sun-Gazette

Officials answer questions at a Thursday news conference in Towanda about the remains of two elderly people found Tuesday in the residence of a relative. From left they are, Cpl. L. Ogden, state police crime unit; Lt. Rick Krawetz, state police; Thomas Carman, Bradford County coroner; and Dan Barrett, Bradford County district attorney.

FIG. 12 THE PRESS CONFERENCE IN TOWANDA, PA.
TAKEN FROM THE SUN GAZETTE, WILLIAMSPORT, PA

After this conference, I couldn't go anywhere locally without being stopped and asked about the case. The news was sensationalized to a great extent. Most people were not upset or appalled at Jean's behavior. Instead, they thought she was just a lonely old person and expressed sympathy for her. This was a relief because it meant less public pressure on me to speed up the investigative process. I was aware that rushing is not suitable during investigations. Taking unnecessary pressure just causes additional stress while dealing with an intense situation. That's why I need to work at a steady pace; I can't skip steps. Admittedly, I was also worried about Jean herself. She was 91, frail (though healthy), and had a clear emotional stake in what the media was hawking over.

On June 17, 2010, the task force ensured that the remains in my morgue were identified correctly. This case was already bizarre, and the idea that Jean had swapped bodies between other graves haunted me. Applying the victimology part of my method required me to get detailed information on the decedents.

I started with the Hartford County Department of Vital Records in Connecticut, who I simply had to subpoena for information regarding the death of June E. Stevens. They were quite accommodating and provided me with the cause, place, and time of death. June died from bladder cancer on October 3rd, 2009, at 20:30. She was 90. She died in Connecticut, where she resided. Subsequently, June was embalmed in Connecticut, then shipped to Pennsylvania to find the Stevens Matson Cemetery. That was the name of the designated site on Jean's property for her burial. The informant on the death certificate was Jean Stevens.

This information is helpful because it supports the idea that June may have favored Jean's odd plans. She wanted to be close to home, so it also validates the witness accounts of the funeral home. People often imagine forensics and death investigation to involve following trails of blood. The reality, we follow both evidence and paths of paper. This is because no investigation can suffice just on shreds of evidence and not on the paperwork.

For Jimmy's records, I contacted Keiper Funeral Home. They provided a death certificate that gave me excellent information. James "Jimmy" Mark Stevens passed on May 21, 1999, at 23:45. He was 86 at the time of his death. In Elmira, NY, Jimmy died in the Arnot Ogden Medical Center (Bradford County borders Chemung County, NY). The cause of death was "Aspiration Pneumonia, Left Hemispheric Cerebrovascular Accident, Multiple Cardio Arterial Embolic Events." The manner of death was natural, and no autopsy was performed. Jimmy was to be buried in the Lime Hill Cemetery that we are so familiar with. Jimmy was embalmed in Elmira, NY, then shipped down to PA. The informant on the death certificate was Jean Stevens. I now know both June and Jimmy had died from natural causes, and thankfully Jean had no part in it.

This second batch of information showed a contrast with June's details. Jimmy wanted to be buried near his brother, not on Jean's property and certainly not stored in her garage on a sofa. So, now I at least knew that one of the two had no intentions of being brought out of the ground and was forced against their will.

The step following my research was to procure medical records from local hospitals. I managed to find some helpful information on Jimmy this way. It turns out he had a rough time health-wise. He had:

- Carotid stenosis (narrowing of important arteries that bring blood to the brain)

- Parkinson's disease

- A history of prostate carcinoma (cancerous tissue in the prostate)

- Peripheral vascular disease

- A hiatal hernia (stomach protruding through the diaphragm)

I also managed to pull information from a VA clinic where Jimmy had been evaluated. Unfortunately, he presented with poor blood circulation in his left arm and was diagnosed with a left brachial artery embolism. He was soon sent to Arnot Ogden, where he died shortly after that. At that point, Jean stayed by his side during his entire hospital stay.

Other records I received indicated that Jimmy had undergone a hemorrhoidectomy, tonsillectomy, adenoidectomy, and prostate resection. Still, there were no implants or anything remotely resembling a serial number verifying that this was Jimmy. This information validates the manner of death, but could I use any of it to verify the remains I had belonged to Jimmy? Tissue identification was not very useful for Jimmy. He was well decomposed. A DNA test wouldn't be possible if I could not find a verifiable sample of Jimmy's DNA to check against. This means that the structures which do not change quickly, the bones and teeth, would be my guiding tools.

I then contacted a local hospital to get dental films (X-rays of the mouth) and had a local dentist, Dr. Joseph Earle, accompany me there. We performed the films at 16:10. Sadly, the jaws of both June and Jimmy were tightly jammed, so I couldn't get perfect movies. Attacking the jaw muscles with surgical tools was an option, but I did not want to, quite literally, deface Jean's relatives just to get a slightly better photo. After that, the images came through, and Dr. Earle informed me there were no unique or notable dental features that would make it easy to check against dental records. Frustrated, I called it a day. I drove the bodies back to the morgue and went to the local tavern to once again relieve my stress. This is a habit that I knew I would eventually quit and find other ways of dealing with mounting stressors. Thankfully, today I remain in sobriety and clean.

The following day, I went to the State Police barracks again and gave them a summary of my investigation. I also gave them copies of the dental films for forwarding to a forensic dentist, Dr. Peter Sellic, in Wyoming County, PA. Dr. Sellic contacted all local dentists in the Wyalusing area requesting records on June or Jimmy if they had any to proceed an inch forward with the case.

Chapter 5

THAT'S NOT
ROSES I SMELL

June 17, 2010. The investigation resumed. This time we focused on the skeletal systems of June and Jimmy. I visited the same radiology department as before, but there were full-body scans in the second attempt of the investigation. At this point, I had not exposed the corpses fully. They were still clothed. As I had already decided not to break their jaws, I considered using the bodies only as much as the investigation required. Actually, a full-body scan does require attention to minor details. So, I removed their clothing. But I was still concerned about clothing zippers or anything metal on their person that could be construed as injury or artifact.

I began this process at 22:09. Jimmy was wearing a white fur hat in the same style as Elmer Fudd, a dark jet-black suit, and blue socks. Around his body were potpourri scented toilet fresheners, layers of newspapers, an afghan, mothballs, layers of paper towels around the neck and chest, a yellow mini pillow, and a cotton ball stuffed into where the nose once was. Jimmy weighed only 50-60 pounds as most of his body had undergone extreme aging decay. He was essentially skin and bones and skeleton-like.

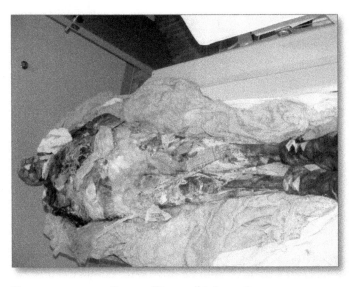

Fig. 13 The remains of James "Jimmy" Mark Stevens prepared for full-body scans on June 21, 2010. Photo by Thomas M. Carman

I requested his body's general A/P view [Anterior/Posterior]. The photos were sent to one Dr. Samsung, who got back to me a few hours later, reporting he found surgical clips in the mid-lower pelvis, a sign pointing toward Jimmy's prostate surgery. This information was valuable to us and gave me a weird sense of relief. Since I knew that since I had concrete evidence proving that this decedent was, in fact, Jimmy, I was confident that the investigation could finally conclude.

The external examination of June occurred at 23:16. Her body had cotton balls and smelled like fingernail polish around the area of her cervical region, meaning inside the vaginal canal and rectum. There were also mothballs within her abdominal cavity that now seemed like a hollow decaying space. She was wearing a red robe, blue pajama bottoms, a blanket, aluminum foil wrapped around the pelvis and abdomen, and mothballs scattered all over. Her face had a makeover, and the entire body had pleasant-smelling perfume doused on it.

June was greatly age decayed. Like Jimmy, she had leathery skin over bone, but her muscle and fat had shrunk down to nearly nothing with dehydration and decay. In addition, there was hazardous mold present that was well developed on the torso and orifices. Although, if I'm going to be totally honest, both Jimmy and June had seen better days; the smell was horrific! Frankly, I was asking myself what in the hell I was doing. Out of all the occupations in the world, I chose to be a Coroner! But then I recalled my love for helping those in need and assisting families on their most horrific days. So, I took a deep breath and believed that there was solid reasoning behind my doings and that of my job.

Scans on June revealed degenerative changes to the lower spine and hip joints. In addition, there was a fracture of the left humeral neck region present. We didn't know if this fracture was antemortem (before death) or postmortem (after death). Truthfully, after being dug from the grave and drug across the yard, postmortem injury was probable.

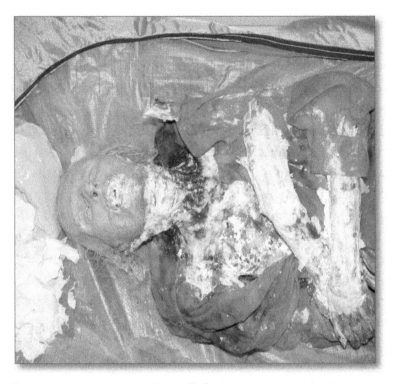

FIG. 14 THE REMAINS OF JUNE E. STEVENS WAS PREPARED FOR A
FULL-BODY SCAN ON JUNE 21, 2010. PHOTO BY THOMAS M. CARMAN

Dr. Samsung also noted a radiopaque material on her teeth visible in the skull scan. This could be a game-changer for dental records if we got ahold of any. The scan could easily help us navigate our way forward in this case too!

Low and behold, we finally have received confirmation that Dr. Sellic was able to positively confirm the identity of both Jimmy and June with dental comparisons that he received and gathered. In addition, I was able to match the surgical clips found within Jimmy. Therefore, we were able to conclude positively that the bodies were both Jimmy and June Stevens. It indeed felt a long haul had finally come to its end.

With the bodies being positively identified, what now? What am I going to do with Jimmy and June? I knew this was going to require tact, skill, and much communication with Jean. And Jean had always been a tough nut to crack, so I knew that getting something out of her would be challenging.

At this point, national media swooned all over this story. I received numerous calls from the Associated Press, Wall Street Journal, LA Times, Chicago Sun-Times, and many other state news outlets. However, the emails that I was receiving from across the world were the most troublesome and genuinely a headache. I had already been pretty wrapped up in this case that the inquiries were just getting on my nerves. Moreover, my inbox was full of assorted emails from both domestic and overseas concerned citizens. These emails were heartfelt and were primarily concerned with Jean's wellbeing and the plan of action. Many emails were far too aggressive for me to discuss here. Most referred to the system and me as bullies and strongarms, cashing out of the whole situation. Unfortunately, they didn't realize this was precisely what I was trying not to be with Jean. I don't like to be a narcissist, but I was the most considerate towards her in this entire investigation.

There were two specific emails that I found to be very interesting. Both were non-threatening. The first had its origin in England, and it went like

"But as far as her psyche, I'll leave that to the experts," referring to a quote I had made to the Associated Press. "Well, perhaps, but I suspect you'll be stuck with lawyers (a crew that is generally confused) and psychologists (I see them as students in my graduate ethics seminars...), and psychiatrists (the best of the bunch, but they tend to think like, well, doctors...) You need a competent, European-trained Existentialist, and I rather doubt you'll find one in your neck of the woods. And if you did, he'd probably be a papist, and that would compromise things differently. I'm afraid the old lady is screwed if you leave things to the experts." Signed "D"

The second, origin Louisiana,

"Mr. Carman, I have just completed my Medicolegal Investigation of Death class at South Louisiana Community College. I am writing to add my support to Jean Stevens. God bless her! In Louisiana, we feel there are 49 states in the United States and then us. We have been savaged by two presidents who will not do anything, BP and hurricane after hurricane. I guess you have seen the rotting flesh on our streets and in the Gulf. Mrs. Stevens has taken better care of her loved ones than what we can do here in Louisiana. So many of our families cannot afford a decent funeral for their loved ones, and I ought to know because I own a funeral home. So please tell Mrs. Stevens she has my support, and I will pray to God to watch over her and her loved ones in life and death." Signed, John Doe.

Sadly, many of our primary counties found humor and disbelief in the situation. Instead, the problem was a grave one and required utmost heed to it. To me, this was anything but humorous. I have an elderly woman who is hell-bent on having her sister and husband back.

The reality of the situation struck me when a man was noticed under my coroner van one day at my office. Not knowing why this unknown man disappeared before anyone recognized or questioned him, our local police chief, Sally Wiselmann, was contacted. My vehicle was taken to a local garage, where it was put on a lift and examined for explosive devices. Thankfully, none were discovered. Yet, to this day, no one knows who this man was or what he was up to. It is seen that very often, such clues are regarded while investigating, but here the whole scene was hushed before it could come into the limelight.

In the meantime, Jean was receiving letters and cards from all around the world. All this attention was keeping Jean smiling, occupied and ignorant. In turn, this was buying me additional time to dive deep into the details. Unfortunately, something was not on my side up to this point. Besides, time was what I required to profile Jean and reach some form of compromise that would be mutually agreeable.

I'll never forget one morning early on meeting with Jean and carrying out a copy of the National Examiner, stating, "We made this magazine." I don't think I will ever forget that beautiful smile that shined through this cloudy situation. That gleam in her eyes showed that she was making sure the world knew that her actions were acceptable and completely justified to be enacted.

Even as an experienced death investigator, I had a brief moment of thinking, oh, what's the big deal? After all, she wasn't abusing June, or for that matter, Jimmy. The only offense was to have them wrapped and placed in storage within the garage. On the other hand, one definitely gets the idea that June is getting her hair brushed, body powdered, and sprayed with perfume. But poor Jimmy, he's getting to rot away while wrapped in newspapers and covered with blankets and a tarp, smelling like a bowl of week-old stale rice.

With the realization of two embalmed bodies further decaying and June leaking fluids, the risk of public health concerns quickly took precedent over kind-heartedness. June and Jimmy deserved and should be placed in the ground, cremated, or placed in a sealed mausoleum. The question is, will Jean agree? Considering she is the person why we are here doing this investigation.

Chapter 6

GOO GOO, GA GA

June 18, 2010. Tpr. Fontelle and I went back to the residence of Jean Stevens. Feeling relieved that Jean had time to realize the severity of the situation, we were hopeful that Jean would be receptive and understand that June and Jimmy belonged somewhere other than her residence. But unfortunately, this was short-lived when Jean immediately asked when she could get June and Jimmy back.

Jean had been dressed as per her own fashion sense. Blouse, skirt, and sneakers were her signature styles, and her hair was fashionably up in a bun. Jean commented, "I could use a handsome funeral director," with a smile on her face, referring to me. Unfortunately, this would be the beginning of long-term abuse by my friends within the state police. Jokingly I would hear, "Oh, the old lady has the hots for you." Later it would become "How is your old girlfriend in Wyalusing?" I was confident enough to say that I will be becoming a banter topic for years to come.

This time a few neighbors joined us at the residence. Noticing our vehicles in front of Jean's house didn't take long for them to approach us. I'll never forget this one old-timer with a handgun on his hip. He stood in the kitchen as if he were there to protect Jean. I can honestly say this Jean had a sound support system with her neighbors, all of which I found to be pleasant. Eventually, I formed a great rapport with many of them throughout my time with Jean for over 18 months.

It wouldn't take long for Tpr. Fontelle and I to come to the realization that Jean was as sane as we are. Although pleased Jean was rational, it undoubtedly complicated things. If we could prove that Jean was suffering from dementia or bat crap crazy, we could have dealt with the remains of June and Jimmy quickly, but this was not the case. Instead, the whole situation was a lot more complicated and puzzling than it seemed. Knowing this would be a long journey, I found comfort in realizing time is the great revealer, and time is what will be required. "Patience" was what I had to hold onto.

Tpr. Fontelle and I began to talk to Jean. We had the advantage of being armed with the knowledge of knowing Jean was suffering from migraines and claustrophobia. Could this claustrophobia be an extremity that would help us explain why June and Jimmy were exhumed from their coffins?

Our conversation with Jean would last a couple of hours before we would depart from her residence. We were stuck at dead-ends and were perturbed, not knowing what we had to do ahead with the remains of June and Jimmy. This would be the last time that anyone would accompany me with future meetings with Jean. I would now be the lone wolf, but the question here imposed was, "Who will win this battle of wits?"

June 19, 2010. My first encounter with Jean solo. At this very moment, I would understand this sweet grandma figure was not the modest, humble, and innocent grandma I assumed she would be. Upon entering her house, I suddenly realized, "Oh no! grandma is not naïve at all!" Three minutes after I entered, I was offered a cup of coffee which I politely refused to. After all, I didn't want to be poisoned! She uttered the following words: "So how about $5000?" I'll give you $5000 if you bring them back. Whoa, I didn't see that coming! I quickly replied to Jean, "That isn't going to happen!" She replied, "I know how these things work." With a burst of hysterical laughter, I replied, "Jean, that can't happen!"

Admittingly, this was quite humorous. The battle of the wits was now on! I had always been accustomed to grandma wits since my grandma Carman was slick herself. I remember when she would make a statement such as, "I can't believe he is marrying that woman." Of course, there was nothing wrong with that statement of hers, but it was that sly way of defending her statement that I used to find amusing.

Sitting at the kitchen table, I hear a familiar sound of subtle gas being passed by Jean. Again, quickly reminded of my grandmother. She would always say, "Wherever thou shall be, let thy wind blow free." Anyways Jean and I began to talk.

Jean started by asking me questions. As an attempt to open a warm conversation, I obliged by answering. Her first question was, "Do you have children? I replied, "Yes." Then, I elaborated that the most precious experience of my life was the birth of our first child.

I explained that my wife and I were at home preparing for bed when I heard, "My water just broke." Talk about reality setting in. Here we go! Emotions of joy, excitement, and anticipation all overwhelmed us at once. The drill sergeant within me came to the forefront. Suddenly I'm barking out orders. "Grab the bag, get in the car." "Are you okay?" "Do you need anything?" and "Let's go!" I blabbered whatever I could at that moment. My wife, already in labor, was ready to strangle me, watching me become a maniac.

I still remember vividly that at the time, we were still about 45 minutes away from the hospital, where prior arrangements had been made for the delivery of Dominic. So, anxiously, we made our way to the car. As you can imagine, the drive was horrific, but we didn't want to stop at a local hospital because our obstetrician was at the other facility. I continuously asked how far apart her contractions were as I mentally prepared myself for the delivery along the side of the road if necessary. Fortunately, we made it safely to the facility. However, thinking that if I had to deliver the baby alongside the road, my wife would've gone nuts at my amateur delivery skills.

Jean asked, "What happened next?"

I continued to tell her that upon our arrival, the paramedics quickly took us to a private room to spend the next two days. When we first arrived, the nurses came in, assessed, and within a few minutes, the obstetrician was at her bedside, and the spectacular show was underway.

"Were you nervous?" Jean asked.

"Oh boy, the anticipation was driving me crazy," I continued. "Suddenly, there was crowning, and I was traveling from my wife's side to the foot of the bed to look at my son's dark, full head of hair. Before I knew it, Dominic's head was out, and the rest of his body soon followed."

Jean asked, "Were you proud?"

I replied, "Proud is an understatement. I'll never forget that new baby smell and the very first cry from what was obviously a healthy set of lungs. While holding my son, the proud father moment kicked in. The emotion of happiness and pride was within me. However, it didn't take long for me to realize that changing diapers sucked," I continued talking to Jean as I saw her comfort level slowly rise.

Jean laughed.

"My wife laughed at me. She used to say that I could deal with dead bodies but couldn't handle a stinky diaper. Don't get me wrong, I was happy to see my son, a healthy voiding machine, but I disliked the responsibility of changing stinky diapers. The thought of wiping a butt and smelling the odor was utterly disgusting to a fussy person like me."

However, when I look back and now think of John 13:14-15, when Jesus washed the feet of his disciples, which was then considered a task of the poorest servants, and informs us that we too shall perform this task was the most humbling action that our Lord performed for our future. This example of love and service establishes that we are all our servants and are no better than the poorest. So, I eventually found neither shame nor disgust in cleaning my flesh and blood.

However, we were not so fortunate with our second son, who experienced bradycardia (slow heart rate), meaning he had to battle between life and death. In addition, it was a dry birth, meaning no amniotic fluid was present, complicating the matter even more. Ultimately, we would find ourselves at the Children's Hospital in Philly. Here we would learn that Terence has Down Syndrome. "Oh, he does," Jean asked. Jean further offered, "I just love those children. There's something incredibly innocent about those kids," Jean exclaimed with her eyes shining as she smiled.

I honestly believed the same as Jean and that everyone should feel lucky to have such an unconditionally loving, demand-limited, smiling baby. Even as he ages, Terence remains with these same qualities. My opinion on changing diapers did not change, however! Upon hearing this, Jean burst into laughter.

After permitting Jean to ask me her first question, I then asked mine. But, of course, this would need to be a mutual open dialect, or my plan would never work.

Since Jean had asked me if I had children, I figured this was an excellent place to start. So, I began to ask, "Do you have any children?" She replied, "No." "Neither June nor I could have children." I replied, "I'm sorry to hear this sad coincidence, Jean."

Please remember I'm accustomed to interviewing within a specific style that directs me to a manner of death. However, in this case, I didn't need to know the manner of death. Instead, I needed to know what to do with June and Jimmy. Besides, I've seen people fighting death up to their last breath and others inviting it in, wittingly or not, but thankfully I have never been in this scenario.

Somewhat winging it, I asked, "So where were you born, Jean?" She replied, "We were born in Philadelphia, Pa. Both June and I. We were twins, you know." Later, I confirmed that both were born on April 13, 1919, in Philly. Then I said, "That must have been neat being a twin." Jean, with a smile, said, "She was my best friend." "We're both claustrophobic, you know?" She spoke as if June was still alive. "We both sleep with the lights on because we're afraid of the dark," Jean informed me. She had never seemed that confident before, considering that she had been explaining a complete hoax.

I received a sudden call from the 911 center. Unfortunately, I had a death to respond to at that time. So, I explained to Jean that I would be back shortly to continue our conversation, which she seemed excited about. "Before you go," Jean asked, "Have you ever had any deaths involving children?"

Being asked to rush by the telephone calls, I replied. "I will tell you about a case I had that was very bizarre with child-like behavior, but now I must get going to this incident."

I remember it was May 12, 2008, a warm spring evening. It was on a Monday. I recall the incident because it was a typical crazy day. I had received a call at 21:58 from the 911 center telling me that I had a self-inflicted gunshot victim to deal with.

So, I responded by turning on music on my way to the crime scene. I always had a strange habit of listening to music on my way to locations, heavy music, plenty of guitar riffs, and powerful vocals. It helps me get in the zone for what I'm about to face and prepare for the investigation. On my way back home, the music varies to the type of incident. If it's a horrific scene, I tend to play softer tunes.

On the other hand, I will usually continue with the heavy riffs on an ordinary natural death. "Oh, this means you're fond of music," Jean replied. "No," I replied. "Not just fond; I love music from the bottom of my heart!"

Then, I arrived at the location to find a single-story mobile home in a remote wooded area. A marked Pennsylvania State Police vehicle and an unmarked car were in the driveway. After photographing the property's exterior, I made my way into the residence.

Although cluttered, the interior was full of cool collectible items in the original boxes. When I say full, I mean floor to ceiling with narrow pathways throughout. As I was sifting, I was intrigued and impressed with the variety of old items and well-preserved packaging. Later, I would learn that the victim's father owned the residence and contents.

Between one section of the contents was a dusty old sofa with a checkered pattern. Something that I would expect to see in an older person's home or cabin. On it lay a middle-aged man who presented supine (on his back). The body was of a 41-year-old white male named Ted Halloway. Upon closer assessment, a handgun was present too. It rested loosely in the right hand of Mr. Halloway.

There was a copious amount of blood that had drained from the nares, ears, and mouth of Mr. Halloway and was now clotted, saturating his shirt and sofa. Blood droplets rained down from his mustache and beard. Two teeth were resting on his outer shirt, which is not an uncommon finding with gunshot head wounds, often resulting from expanding gases and soot from the end of the muzzle.

These expanding gases produce what we refer to as "Blowback." This is a clear indication of close or direct contact of the muzzle against the skin. Generally speaking, the gases enter the wound, expand, and return through the path of least resistance which is often the entrance wound. This will leave residue, along with blood on the muzzle, clothing, and hand of the suicidal actor. As horrifying as it sounds, this was a part of my job, and I had now become accustomed to seeing such horrors.

It was time to gather historical information about the incident after discussing details with Tpr. Pete Frahley, an acting lead investigator with the state police, determined that a gentleman named

George Lawrence had been on location prior to my arrival. Further discussion with Tpr. Frahley revealed that Mr. Lawrence had left the scene to return home to comfort his wife, Catherine.

Mr. Lawrence was the discoverer and 911 caller. Coincidently, he initially came to the residence to confront and have an altercation with Mr. Halloway. Still, after pounding on the door with no response, he carefully peeked through a small window to see what he believed to be Mr. Halloway, lifeless, on the sofa.

We examined a cell phone that was near Mr. Halloway on the floor. This was when the case finally started to get very interesting. We also discovered a text that had been sent by Mr. Halloway to Ms. Lawrence, alluding to the fact that perhaps Mr. Halloway and Ms. Lawrence were more than just friends. However, there was clearly a suicidal ideology present within the text.

Thankfully, a suicide note was present. Social media apps have become the new age of suicide notes. Facebook, Tinder, Grindr, and a host of other platforms are very revealing. Simply put, the new wave suicide note is often a text or discovered on a social media platform. Millennials find social media apps to have better reach and accessible platforms to put their thoughts on, thus being preferred mediums of suicidal notes.

The scene was processed, and Mr. Halloway was placed in a body bag. The examination and toxicology studies would be done at the morgue later after crucial interviews were conducted.

Now it's time to digest the text message and follow up with good interviews. There is, without doubt, an etiology foundation for this sudden, unexplained action of self-destruction. So, what is it?

Our standard practice is to interview individuals separately. We have found that this achieves a much more quality interview with better results. Experience has taught us that interviewing people collectively only results in the hesitation of information provided and, at best, limited information. Grouped interviews are also widely acclaimed for the Hawthrone effect amongst the ones interviewed. For example, if the husband and wife are being interviewed together, one or the other may be resistant to discuss certain things that could be detrimental to the case. Fear or protective factors could discourage one party from speaking openly with the other present.

Nevertheless, the interview with Mr. Lawrence went very well. We would learn that Mr. Halloway has been a family friend for the past several years. He would visit their home frequently, spending quality time attending cookouts, holidays, and family parties.

Mr. Lawrence described Mr. Halloway as a quiet, withdrawn, and somewhat depressed man. Further stating that Mr. Halloway had been in the military, married at one point, now divorced, and his only son had been killed in a car accident a few years back. Ironically, after the death of his son, Mr. Halloway became friends with the Lawrence's.

Suddenly, the tone of Mr. Lawrence's voice changed. His facial expression changed to that of a frustrated man. At this point, we knew Mr. Lawrence had information that would shed valuable light on this incredibly dark situation.

After that, Mr. Lawrence abruptly came out with what he was hiding. "Listen," he said, "Halloway has been getting friendly with my wife!" He went on to say they have been getting closer over the past few weeks and that it pissed him off. Mr. Lawrence then states, "Halloway left suddenly tonight and then sends a text to my wife." Finally, Mr. Halloway, without hesitation, says, "Honestly, I went to the trailer tonight to kick his ass, but then I saw him." As an investigator, we refer to clearing the smoke and mirrors, revealing the truth.

Surprisingly, the interview with Ms. Lawrence went equally well. Ms. Lawrence confirmed that Mr. Halloway had, in fact, been getting much friendlier with her over the past several weeks. However, we never did ascertain if they were sexually intimate at any point throughout their friendship. Honestly, it was not relevant to the investigation, and I never believed in wasting time enquiring about insignificant things.

What was relevant was what happened today. Ms. Lawrence enlightened us on today's activities. First, Mr. Halloway frankly asked her to leave her husband. Mr. Halloway told Ms. Lawrence, "He doesn't love you the way you deserve!" "We can escape together and go on a treasure hunt." Halloway even suggested that they should get married. It was at this moment that Ms. Lawrence stated that she asked Mr. Halloway to leave the residence and never return!

Evidence discovered on the cell phone became very clear. Critical verbiage was found, such as, "I'm lonely," "I'm heartbroken," "I want to return your heart to you," and "The treasure hunt is over." Now the motive for suicide was becoming clearer.

Now that we have a motive, we need to prove two key things to confirm this was a self-inflicted injury.

Was Halloway physically capable of performing the act?

Is the injury pattern consistent with suicide versus the action of another?

This will be answered at the morgue by further examination and testing.

Jean had a confused look on her face. I interjected, "Jean, I would assume you're wondering what any of this has to do with a child." "Yes," I was wondering," Jean replied. "I'm going to take you to the examination table with me at the morgue to help you get a clearer view." "Okay," she replied.

Imagine Halloway now in front of us on the examination table. He measures 70 inches in length and weighs 228 pounds. His hair is brown with gray highlights measuring 8cm in length and is blood-soaked with copious amounts of clotted blood with some brain matter presenting. His pupils are brown in color and are dilated, round, equal, and fixed. The sclera (whites of the eyes) is free from jaundice discoloration and petechiae (pinpointing hemorrhages). Teeth are natural and in relatively good condition. The skull presents with evident crepitation from the underlying bony structures being disturbed from the injury.

"We must rebuild the skull and face. This is common with high-powered long guns or shotguns. Commonly these injuries produce bony fragments, along with tissue destruction and often a blown-out empty skull cavity."

"Are you with me, Jean?" I asked. "Oh yes," Jean replied. I continued, "Halloway used a handgun which tends to be kinder to the skull and face. Don't get me wrong, but we still tend to find bony fractures; however, they're generally in place under the skin. In either case, we are generally able to get the facial tissue back into place and search for injury evidence establishing the distance of the shot."

"Oh my," Jean replies. Halloway's skull was intact, and the integrity of the head and face were left unaltered except for palpable bony irregularities, as mentioned earlier.

The entrance wound is clearly established under the chin. In addition, there is powder and an abrasion ring under the chin. An abrasion ring is a predominately circular area indicative of an entrance wound of direct contact. This is caused by the impact of the bullet on the skin and the stretching that occurs. However, the soot's can usually be washed away; whereas, an abrasion collar cannot be removed.

Now we must measure the arm. The arm length is crucial in these cases, along with the weapon's size. Here, Halloway's arm measures 29 inches in length. His right hand has both gun powder and blowback (blood and tissue). Halloway used a handgun, so obviously, he was able to self-administer the fatal injury.

We must now itemize and catalog the clothing. Halloway had on a pair of generic white sneakers, which were removed. Socks are white, and they are released. Next, we pulled a long sleeve shirt, and here is where we got engrossed.

Halloway has on what we initially believe to be a tee-shirt. It's white and has the word "Pampers" across the front. However, when we remove his Wrangler blue Jeans, to our disbelief, we see it is an adult onesie. Yes, an adult onesie! It even has snaps within the crotch region. "What!" Jean exclaims. "Oh yes," I state.

"It gets better, Jean," after unsnapping the onesie, we discover a pink-colored adult diaper. I must confess this was a first for me. I have seen plenty of "Depends" type diapers on medically dependent victims but never a colored diaper for pleasure. Upon hearing further, Jean sat silent.

After digesting this image for a bit and not knowing whether to laugh or cry, I came to a realization that I was confused as to why an adult would be wearing a diaper and onesie. As I established previously, I dislike changing diapers. However, here it goes! Time to humble me and remove the darn diaper!

The diaper is saturated with urine. The tricky part is determining whether this was an antemortem (prior to death), perimortem (during death), or post-mortem (after death) event. Besides, it's certainly not uncommon to release urine and occasionally defecate at the time of death. In fact, with trauma-related deaths, it's not unusual to find ejaculated semen.

So far, examination, photography, and blood have been collected for toxicology studies. Jean asked, "Why was he wearing a pink diaper?" "I had to do some research," I replied. My mind was racing, and honestly, I was curious why this man found pleasure in wearing a onesie and diaper. It was pretty curious for his age.

"What did you find out?" Jean asked. "Jean, I often pray for wisdom, and this was no exception. But I need to forewarn you that prayer comes with results. So, learn to expect the unexpected! I turn to scripture for comfort at such times." I told her. "Oh," Jean replies. This is something I have been doing a lot of since meeting Jean. I was learning as much as Jean was learning throughout this situation.

I asked Jean, "Do you know what 2 Peter 3:10-14 says?" Jean replied, "No."

"Well, I didn't either, Jean, but it says, *'but the day of the Lord will come like a thief. Therefore, be diligent to be found by Him without spot or blemish and at peace.'*"

I continued, "I need to be honest with you. When I read this, all I could think of was, how would you like to be found by Jesus in an adult onesie with a pink diaper on? I know it's wrong, but honestly, it's the first thing that came to mind." Jean laughed.

I had to do some research. I hit the books and researched online. I personally had to know what this fetish was all about for this case and any future cases that my office may investigate.

I learned much more than I wanted to, so I knew what I needed to learn. I must say Google is one heck of an educational tool for research. What I found was both informative and exciting, at least for investigative purposes.

I discovered that most "diaper lovers" ironically do not like to engage in infantile activity, but go figure this out at your own risk! Getting fed by a bottle, someone changing their diapers, and being rocked doesn't interest most diaper fetish participants. Consequently, I limited my research to the non-infantile adult diaper wearers. I did this because I was already horrified by people's unusual fetishes and lusts.

"Why exactly would anyone want to participate in this unique lifestyle," she asked. The American Psychological Association recognizes this behavior. I couldn't find when this behavior started, but there is clear evidence that in the 70s, groups of diaper wearers began coming together.

I found that the act of adult diaper-wearing (non-medicinal purposes) can be both non-sexual and sexual. For example, the non-sexual interest revolves around comfort, coziness, the need to feel cared for, the feeling of being safe, fear of bedwetting, traumatic experience during potty training, and some wearers psychologically want to shed the responsibility of adulthood. Likewise, the opposite is for sexual satisfaction, which can revolve around the sensation of wearing or watching someone else wear a diaper and/or wetting it. Sometimes the humiliation of wearing the diaper, or making someone else wear the diaper, is sexually satisfying incredibly in the sexual masochism arena.

Whether non-sexual or sexual, it is physically and psychologically gratifying to the wearer. Believe it or not, there are thousands upon thousands of adult diaper wearers in the world. I'm not kidding you. In Chicago, there's a business that opened that caters specifically to this group of fetish members. I noted online that not only does this store sell adult diapers of a multitude of colors and patterns, it also sells adult cribs, adult highchairs, and a host of other items. Jean shook her head, and we laughed together.

During my Google research, I stumbled upon a diaper-wearing fetish group column. So, I did the most logical thing. I went creeping, lol. But, of course, Jean had no idea what I meant by that.

Undoubtedly, the most significant thing I took from the column was the statement by an unidentified woman, "As with all fetishes, you get it when you have it, and you don't get it when you don't have it." So, in the kink scene, we say, "Your kink isn't my kink, but your kink is okay."

Chapter 7

WHO STANDS
BEFORE ME?

06/21/2010, three days have gone by since I last spoke with Jean. After our last open dialogue, I felt confident that Jean and I were making progress that would lead to closure soon. Today's main objective was to get June and Jimmy out of my office and keep them where they should rightfully be. This could only be achieved by learning more about who Jean is.

The goal is to find out as much as I can about Jean and her loved ones and win her emotionally. This is precisely what today's mission will be. The ride out was fantastic—a lovely sunny day, great for driving. My window was down, music cranked up, coffee in hand. In a very long time, today felt good. I was positive that Jean was in a position where she would be open to discussing June and Jimmy's final disposition.

Jean is in the doorway with a smile on her face. This time when offered, I accepted a cup of coffee. I had reached a point of comfortability with Jean. I was convinced she wouldn't try to poison me. "I have something to tell you," Jean said, grinning from ear to ear. Thinking maybe she would inform me that she had come up with a conclusion, I said, "What's that?" "I was watching late-night television, and Leno mentioned it to me." "Oh yeah," I replied. "Yes," he said something about the lady from Wyalusing, PA., living with her dead relatives. Now I was nervous about progress. It appears that Jean loves this attention. This made today's interview or chat a need at that time. I had to discover what Jean was truly up to.

I started by saying, "Jean, I really need to ask you a few questions today." Jean said, "Sure!" "First, tell me about your childhood." I started with my question. "Well, June and I were twins born in Philadelphia on April 13, 2019," Jean replied. I said, "Yes, I remember you telling me that." My father was Glen Elbridge Burnham Matson. My mother was Bertha Planton Matson. My father died of lung cancer in 1950. My mother died of TB and pneumonia.

Jean went on to say, "My mother died when I was 30. She died in 1949. She was 57." I knew for a fact as I had already looked at the headstone of Bertha P. Matson in the Lime Hill Cemetery. Jean asked, "Can I tell you something?"

I replied, "Go ahead."

"After my mother died, Jimmy and I went to Florida, but I refused to go unless I could see my mother." Jean made a revelation.

"To see your mother," I asked.

"Yes, I told Jimmy I wouldn't go unless I could see my mother," she replied.

"What really happened?" I asked.

"We stopped at the cemetery, and we dug my mother's grave up."

"Really?"

"Yes, we dug her up, and I sat with her for a while." "What did Jimmy do?" I asked.

"He waited for me, and then we left for Florida!"

"Did you remove your mother from her casket" I pondered and then chose to ask her directly.

"No, I just looked at her. She was beautiful, you know." "How long was this after she died," I asked.

"Around two months," Jean replied. "We closed the casket, which was a beautiful "Coach casket."

"What is a coach casket?" I asked, "It was beautiful, and there was a full-length body view. She donned a beautiful dress, and her hair was beautiful. I was in school when she got sick." "I'm sorry to hear this," I replied.

Now curious if this was Jean's first dig, I asked, "Jean was this the first time you dug a grave up?" Jean replied, "Yes, and I haven't dug my mother up again yet!" "Yet?" I thought for a moment, deciding that I wasn't even going to go there. After all, I knew exactly what Jean's intent was. The only image I had was of a house full of dead corpses sitting all over in the place. A reality show of house horrors. At that point, even old Jimmy would be in the house to join the party.

I quickly moved on to my next question. "What about your father? Have you ever dug him up?" I asked. "No," I was going to but didn't because the cemetery had a caretaker, so he's protected. He's buried in the Camp town cemetery, you know." Suddenly, Jean got sidetracked and started talking about when she visited a hospital with her mother in her childhood. "They needed to get an x-ray of me. They told me they were going to take a picture. I asked them, "Shall I smile"? Jean laughed as she told me this.

I asked Jean about her childhood. She expressed to me that they moved around a lot. Jean stated, "My dad was a salesman. He worked for Woolworths and later started his own company. June and I were very close. She was my best friend, you know."

With very little doubt in my mind that her narrative was invalid, I smiled.

I was trying to change the subject momentarily out of habit (an effective tool for reducing the likelihood of a pre-rehearsed statement). "It must have been quite an undertaking getting Jimmy from the cemetery to your house," I asked.

"Yes, I had a few friends help me," she replied. "Friends?" I asked.

"Yes, don't worry, they're all dead now," Jean replied with a smile.

FIG. 15 FROM LEFT TO RIGHT, JEAN STEVENS, GLEN MATSON, BERTHA MATSON, AND JUNE STEVENS. PHOTO CREDIT- JEAN STEVENS

"How did you get him from there to here?" I inquired, unsettled by her latest answer.

Jean replied, "In my station wagon."

"The one in the garage?"

"Yes," she replied.

I smirked, deeming it interesting.

We had established who assisted with the digging up of June previously on day one, but I still didn't know how they got her to the house and inside.

"How did you get June from the grave to the house?"

"It wasn't easy!" she replied. "The grave was full of water, you know."

"Oh, that must have been a mess," I said.

"Yes, it was. We put her on a sled and brought June to the house," Jean replied.

"How did you get her into the spare bedroom?"

"We carried her," she replied.

FIG. 16 JEAN AND JUNE STEVENS. PHOTO CREDIT -JEAN STEVENS

I had a difficult time picturing anyone assisting with this absurd chore. When the individual was questioned, he replied that he saw Jean digging and was worried about Jean having a heart attack. Sadly, the media deemed and referred to him as the "Lime Hill Body Snatcher." To me, he was just narrating the horror his eyes had witnessed on the day of the digging.

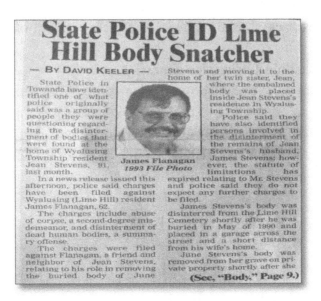

State Police ID Lime Hill Body Snatcher

— By David Keeler —

State Police in Towanda have identified one of what police originally said was a group of people they were questioning regarding the disinterment of bodies that were found at the home of Wyalusing Township resident Jean Stevens, 91, last month.

In a news release issued this afternoon, police said charges have been filed against Wyalusing (Lime Hill) resident James Flanagan, 62.

The charges include abuse of corpse, a second-degree misdemeanor, and disinterment of dead human bodies, a summary offense.

The charges were filed against Flanagan, a friend and neighbor of Jean Stevens, relating to his role in removing the buried body of June

James Flanagan
1993 File Photo

Stevens and moving it to the home of her twin sister, Jean, where the embalmed body was placed inside Jean Stevens's residence in Wyalusing Township.

Police said they have also identified persons involved in the disinterment of the remains of Jean Stevens's husband, James Stevens; however, the statute of limitations has expired relating to Mr. Stevens and police said they do not expect any further charges to be filed.

James Stevens's body was disinterred from the Lime Hill Cemetery shortly after he was buried in May of 1990 and placed in a garage across the street and a short distance from his wife's home.

June Stevens's body was removed from her grave on private property shortly after she

(See, "Body," Page 9.)

FIG. 17 "Lime Hill Body Snatcher" from the Rocket-Courier

I knew I needed to ask Jean, so I did, "Why was Jimmy in the garage and June in the house?" Upon hearing my question, Jean's facial expression changed to that of a straight face. "Because I liked her more," she replied. This would be the first time Jean used "Like" instead of "Love" when she talked about June.

With our limited conversation about June, I already realized a deep platonic love between Jean and June. Love is a beautiful gift from God. In fact, we are instructed over 50 times throughout the New Testament to love one another. Love is not an emotion. It is not an option. Love is a commandment. Love is the purest of all feelings. Christ commands us to love one another, and this is how the world will know we belong to Christ. There are a few easy steps to love. Start within the church, then outside of our home, and finally within our homes. Call me a pessimist, but I don't feel that Jesus meant that this love should consist of co-residing with a dead corpse. So, love can be anything, but not unlawful.

"Jean, I noticed at the cemetery June had a headstone. However, Jimmy did not," I asked with suspicion.

"I never bought one," she replied. Then, smirking, Jean said, "The lady from the cemetery asked when I was going to get one, but I thought, why get a tombstone when he isn't in there!" I laughed. This was the first time I realized that Jean was full of wit. At that moment, we started to bond. With her presence in the room, I couldn't help but think of my own grandmother. Jean was a beautiful reminder of her.

Retracting to Jimmy.

"Jean, tell me about Jimmy." She proceeded to tell me that Jimmy was born on 07/05/1912 in Factoryville, Pa., and later served in the army from 1942-1946, fighting in WWII at the Battle of the Bulge. A war that Sir Winston Churchill would state, "This is undoubtedly the greatest American battle of the war and will, I believe, be regarded as an ever-famous American victory." Indeed, in terms of participation and losses, the Battle of the Bulge is arguably the greatest in American military history.

Jean went on to tell me that when Jimmy got out of the army, he would eventually work for General Electric as an Aviation Machinist. "June and I married brothers," you know. Jimmy's brother is "Kemp." His real name is Allison, but we call him Kemp. He is two years older than Jimmy.

FIG. 18 JEAN STEVENS AND HUSBAND, JAMES STEVENS.
PHOTO CREDIT- JEAN STEVENS.

I found it interesting that while Jean discussed her loved ones, she referred to them as they still existed. She would use the word "Is" as if they were alive and with her. I strongly felt that she had not come to terms with the death of her loved ones. Later I would learn that Allison "Kemp" Stevens died on December 11, 1993. And some six years later, On May 21, 1999, Jimmy died. This would leave June and Jean alone. Their twin sisterly bond and love grew more profound as they found solace in each other's company.

"Jean, when I was at the cemetery, I couldn't help but notice that Kemp and June have a plot with a headstone and both their names on it," I said. As Jean heard me, she quickly interrupted me and started saying, "I promised June I would never leave her side."

It felt like she was angered by my question and was becoming defensive about her actions. "We can talk about that later," I replied. Not wanting to upset Jean, I thought that this was enough for one day. But I couldn't help but wonder whether they collectively had this worked out and planned it. Although illegal, unsanitary, and unsafe, was this really the plan?

FIG. 19 "KEMP" AND JUNE STEVENS HEADSTONE
IN THE LIME HILL CEMETERY. PHOTO BY THOMAS M. CARMAN

As I left Jean's home, I had the music cranked up, but I couldn't get the conversation with Jean out of my mind. It itched to think if there was not a selfish motive here. This was important for me to know. I firmly believe that self-centered living will not let you enjoy the true gift of life. Imagine if this was all done out of love and a promise to June? As I previously mentioned, this doesn't make it legal, and getting June and Jimmy back is out of the question too.

Honestly, it's bothering me that people are referring to Jean as the "Crazy old lady from Wyalusing." But, from the point I'm looking at her from, she is far from crazy. Eccentric, possessive, and possibly controlling might have better described her, but it's too early to tell.

However, I remain adamant that a time will come when June and Jimmy will have a proper final burial. In the meantime, both will stay in the morgue in my office. What is strange is that I find myself introducing June and Jimmy to other decedents as I place them in the cooler. After all, it has been six days that they have been with me.

Speaking to the dead is no new habit to me. It is pervasive for me to say a few words to those that come to the morgue. Praying for them is what I practice regularly. To the young that have expired, I apologize that the event happened to them. Strange, but this is the only way I deal with death.

Although the dead doesn't literally speak back to me, they do talk through their blood, traumatic injuries, and/or natural anatomical abnormalities. It is their voice that will lead me to a cause and manner of death. Based on the odor emitting from my cooler, it would appear that June and Jimmy were telling me to get them cremated, buried, or placed in a mausoleum soon. I wish I could help their poor souls in some way!

Chapter 8

HMM, IS THAT BEEF STEW?

The following week I pulled up to Jean's house and got out with a cigarette in my hand. This time I got busted. "Don't you know those things are bad for your health," said Jean. No matter how much I wanted to say so is collecting embalmed bodies, but that wouldn't have been nice, would it? So, I smiled and said, "I know Jean, I'm going to quit."

After inviting me into the house, Jean said. "I remember you saying I remind you of your grandmother. Why is that? Did she dig up graves too?" She asked while laughing. I replied, "No, Jean, she didn't, but she lived in a rural community just like you. She had a wit about her like you. She also had a garden and enjoyed fresh produce just like you. I casually slipped in details and similarities that my grandmother and Jean had, thinking it would warm the conversation before I got down to business.

I reminisced, "We're really blessed when it comes to fresh produce. The number of fresh vegetables and locally grown fruits is exceptional. From mint greens to apples, the plants are abundant. One of my personal favorite fruits grown locally are bountiful, deliciously flavored tomatoes.

Our last home had a large garden spread over approximately 30 feet by 80 feet. It was a tiny garden in the scheme of things, but it was our own. We kept it fenced in to keep the wildlings out. We were thoroughly impressed by the produce, and to celebrate it, we sang all glory and praise to God. Our plants did well, and we had a luscious harvest. My wife would bottle and freeze the harvest to preserve them. Then, she would make fresh jams out of them." "Oh yes, that is something I would do too," Jean replied.

I nodded as though agreeing with her, "When I think about those times, I cherish fond memories of my grandmother's garden. She had a decent-sized tomato plot out back of her old house. So, we would pick tomatoes. Then, after handpicking the tomatoes carefully, we used to wash all the dirt on them.

My grandmother and mother did the task of washing those bad boys and prepping them for canning. Soon there would be spaghetti gravy simmering on the stove to make pasta."

"Hmm, that sounds good," Jean replied.

Laughing, I said, "Yes, the trail of tomato puree would be all over the counter and walls. We would happily eat fresh spaghetti gravy for weeks. It was preferred for the pasta and chicken and other condiments to be cooked to perfection. Besides, it is true how you just can't beat fresh tomato marinara." "You sure can't," Jean testified.

You know there's an old proverb that I'm sure you have heard. "Give a man a fish, and you feed him for a day. Teach him how to fish, and you feed him for a lifetime." For years I thought this derived from scripture. But, honestly, it's actually a quote from an old Chinese philosopher Lao Tzu who was the founder of Taoism.

The Bible tells us what is ours to eat. God said, "I give you every seed-bearing plant on the face of the whole earth and every tree that has fruit with seed in it. They will be yours for food. Later in scripture, it says, "Everything that lives and moves about will be food for you. Just as I gave you the green plants, I now give you everything." God knows that our flesh is weak. So, it only makes sense that mankind would push the boundaries and limits. Jean nodded in agreement.

This was the perfect time for me to interject a case, so I presented it as a story with Jean. "Let me tell you about this one case I had."

She listened intently and exclaimed, "I like your stories."

It was a relatively warm day. I had just finished up a case at a local hospital. Wrapping up the case, I jumped into my vehicle and turned the air conditioner on, looking forward to a nice ride back to the office. Suddenly, my phone rings. It was a longtime friend, a paramedic with a local ambulance service. Unknown to me, they had been dispatched to a scene in one of our rural towns.

After answering, my friend says, "Tom, you need to come out to this scene!" Now, mind you, this is a paramedic with many years of experience and a tough cookie to crumble. So, when he informs me that I better come out to a scene, I know undoubtedly that we have an incident that will be both extensive and complex.

"No problem, I'm 25 minutes away," I assured him. Then, he proceeded to brief me about his concerns. His following words were both exciting and concerning. "Tom, I have a lady down and a man here that states he had sex with this dead woman." "Now, this can mean a variety of things to me. Please clarify that." I replied with utter confusion. "Do you mean they were having sex and she died, or do you mean he had sex with a dead woman?" His reply was, "He had sex with a corpse!" Oh boy, is the scene safe? I asked. His answer was priceless: "Yeah, unless you're a dead woman!"

I had to laugh. But what else could I've done, cry? You just can't make this stuff up. Hundreds of death investigations, but this was a first for me. As coroners, we see things that would give most people nightmares. There were two cases of a brother and sister who were 6 and 7, drawing on their naked dead mother's body with a permanent blue marker while she lay dead in bed, and a little girl with pneumonia who died as a result of her parents refusing to give her an antibiotic because they refused modern medicine.

I spent the next 20 minutes driving, listening to Rob Zombie, which I thought was appropriate based on the information I had just learned. I try listening to artists that coincide with whatever the incident is.

As I'm driving, I'm painfully thinking about necrophilia. Sexual intercourse with or an attraction to a corpse, an act as disgusting as it sounds. In fact, Merriam-Webster defines necrophilia as an "Obsession with and usually erotic interest in or stimulation by corpses."

"Wow! You see some interesting things!" Jean asked. "What were you thinking on your way there?"

The thought that kept entering my brain was Jeffrey Dahmer. He was a serial killer who performed necrophilia. The truth is many non-serial killers commit this act. In fact, many more than we would like to think about. A quick example is that of a young woman named Karen Greenlee. Ms. Greenlee was 22 at the time and worked as an apprentice embalmer in Sacramento, California. Documents state that after spending two days with a dead 33-year-old man's corpse, she tried to commit suicide by overdosing on pills. During the investigation, police discovered a five-page letter. Within it, Ms. Greenlee confessed to having previously slept with at least 20 to 40 dead men.

One of the fascinating cases of necrophilia actually occurred in Key West, Florida, in the early 1900s. Carl Tanzler, a German Immigrant, settled in Florida, working in the medical profession. In short, Tanzler met a young woman named Maria Elena Milagro de Hoyos and fell in love. As she presented with tuberculosis, Tanzler was convinced this was his true love and soulmate. Sadly, she died shortly after that.

On an April evening in 1933, nearly two years after her death, Tanzler removed her body from the mausoleum and transported it on a toy wagon back to his home. Interestingly, Tanzler reattached the bones using coat hangers, made fake skin, and replaced the eye balls with doll eyes. He then co-resided with his love for seven years before being caught, losing his love and sexual partner. "Why would anyone want to do that?" Jean asked. I assumed she was referring to the act of sex with a dead body and not the removal of the corpse from a mausoleum.

A shrug was all I could manage as the answer to her question.

"When I arrived on the scene, I noted an isolated house, with the closest home in the vicinity being some quarter of a mile away. It would appear from a distance that this was an old farmhouse with the skeletal remains of an old barn across the road. Other than weathered wood with roof collapse, nothing remained there – a common site in our county.

It was difficult to see the driveway with just a tire path with grass growing in the middle of what was once a driveway. However, I spotted an ambulance at the top, knowing it was the correct location.

The house was a now faded yellow residence with an extremely weathered shingled roof. I could appreciate that this was once a beautiful property. The house sits amid a large yard. I use the word yard giving it the benefit of the doubt. It is more like a hay field in drastic need of mowing and trimming. The grass is a good 12 inches or higher.

Sitting in the front seat of the ambulance is my friend shaking his head in disbelief. The state police arrived shortly after that. The patrol officer immediately secures the scene by placing yellow tape around the home, ensuring the tape is wrapped around relatively close trees.

I notice a middle-aged man sitting on the front porch cement steps. Trooper Candish, a criminal investigator with the state police, pulls in and parks. Tpr. Candish and I have worked on many cases together over the years. Together, we approach the male subject sitting on the steps.

He is a slender-faced man with cheeks sunken in. A pair of plastic-framed, large glasses covering a large area of his face is on his face. His face is covered with several days of brown/gray whiskers that he has outgrown. His teeth are tobacco-stained, and, likely, he hasn't seen a toothbrush in weeks. His head is balding with just short hair on the sides and back. He's wearing a dirty pair of blue Jeans, a dirty tee-shirt, and an old pair of dirty, white in color, generic brand sneakers. In his hand, a thin cigar was burning. He had apparent tremors, with his hands shaking badly.

When asked his name and age, he replied, "Johnnie Wakefield, 42 years old." Mr. Wakefield had a slurred speech pattern and distinguishing stutter with a delayed response to questions. His speech pattern and shakes made it apparent that Mr. Wakefield was on some form of behavioral altering medication, be it legal or illegal.

After explaining to Mr. Wakefield that we would need to process the residence room by room, he provided verbal consent. After being asked for a general overview of what took place, Mr. Wakefield referred to a lady that lay on the floor and died. All we did was ask for a general overview, but this is precisely what we received. So, now our work became easier since we would have all the hassle cut out for us.

We entered the back-enclosed porch first. This was an approximate 6x8 area. For lack of any other fitting words, it was atrocious! Garbage bags full of old trash scattered around, mixed with piles of dirty clothes. Interestingly enough, there was a brand-new white chest freezer near the wall. Confused, I noticed a large roll of gauze-type material that was 4 inches in width and lay on top of the freezer.

We then proceeded inside. This took us directly into the kitchen. Dirty dishes were piled in the sink, some with food still on them. The floors in the entire downstairs and the upstairs were worn and had wide-planked barn boards. I can only imagine how beautiful this floor was in its day.

There was an opening that resembled a window without glass between the kitchen and living room. There was a shelf at the bottom of the opening. Suddenly, something caught my eye. I immediately froze. As I drew closer, I realized it was a rubber sex toy on the shelf. It was red in color. A second rubber toy caught my eye as I turned and looked on top of the refrigerator. This was purple in color. Although I have certainly seen sex toys in other residences while investigating, I had never seen any in a kitchen.

We then entered a large living room. Describing this as disorderly would be an under-statement. Multiple piles of newspapers, magazines, personal property, and garbage were strewn about. In the corner of the living room was an older computer desk. On it was a computer, some papers, and a box of Kleenex. Also present on the computer desk was a container of personal lubricant. In the wastebasket next to the computer were tons of Kleenex that had a substance on them. On one end of the table in the middle of the room were two garden carrots, approximately 8 to 9 inches in length. Tpr. Candish and I looked at each other and, in synchrony, said, 'I don't even want to know.'

Making our way across the living room, we discover the body of a female victim. The body lay on the living room floor adjacent to a downstairs bathroom. The female presents nude and supine (on her back). She is a large woman (later determined to be 355 pounds). Her legs were spread wide open, and fluid was noted to be within the genital region. There was no external trauma pointed out at a quick glance. The cervical region (neck) is assessed quickly for ligature marks. None were noted. We decided to continue mapping the house before further examining it. After a while, another sex toy is found when the bathroom is examined.

We went up a wooden stairway to process the upstairs. The upstairs was pretty much in the same disarray as the downstairs. Upon entering the bedroom, a dresser and queen-size bed were noted. There were other rubber sex toys on the dresser top, along with additional rolls of the same gauze-type material found at the top of the freezer downstairs. There's a nightstand next to the bed with different personal lubricants and two extra garden carrots, measuring exactly 8 to 9 inches like the ones discovered downstairs."

"This guy really likes carrots," Jean said innocently.

I sighed and nodded. I refrained from detailing there and then why he was using the carrots.

I continued, "Disgusted, we analyzed the bed. There was a bare, dirty, stained mattress with a raunchy, single sheet on top. A pillow lay at the top of the bed. Interestingly, each bedpost had that same gauze-type material that we noted previously tied around it. It was very much possible that we were amid a very sexually active residence. Bondage would be the least of activities, I assumed.

Now came the time for the inevitable, the interview. We had made the decision to interview Mr. Wakefield before completing scene processing and body movement.

Interviewing Mr. Wakefield was time-consuming and challenging due to his tremors and speech pattern. But, note, we were sympathetic, discovering from medical records inside the desk that Mr. Wakefield suffers from depression, anxiety, and schizophrenia.

Admittingly, we initially thought this guy couldn't possibly be sexually active with all the behavioral medication he is taking; however, upon discovering a small jar filled with Viagra, we realized that this would be possible," Jean had her eyes fixated on me as she listened carefully to the account I detailed.

According to Mr. Wakefield, a female by the name of Laura arrived at his home yesterday morning. She doesn't drive but was able to catch a ride with a friend. Laura suffered from the same behavioral conditions as Mr. Wakefield. We would also learn from Mr. Wakefield that Laura is married but comes to visit for sexual rendezvous. According to Mr. Wakefield, "She is a wild thing that likes it rough."

We asked Mr. Wakefield, "Mr. Wakefield, what did you two do sexually?"

"Well, we liked bondage and toys."

I immediately asked, "Did this include suffocation or anything around the neck." Mr. Wakefield replied, "No, we didn't do anything painful. She wasn't into that," Mr. Wakefield continued, "When she arrived yesterday, we had sex all day! Last night she came downstairs, and when I came down, she was lying in front of the bathroom." When I asked if she was breathing. He replied, "I don't know."

Now was a good time to approach critical questions. "So, what did you do when you saw her laying there?" Keep in mind, that when we initially examined the body, she presented in rigor mortis. Meaning she had been dead for several hours.

Mr. Wakefield responds, "I tried to roll her over, but she was too big. I didn't want her to choke. "Then what happened next?"

"Well, I had sex with her," he replied.

"Did she respond?"

"No, but I think she liked it."

"Why do you think she liked it, Mr. Wakefield?"

"Well, she didn't tell me to stop."

"Mr. Wakefield, Laura has clearly been dead for several hours. Why didn't you call 911?"

"I don't know. I went up to the bed," he replied.

"When you got up this morning, what happened?" He replied, "I got up late in the morning, came down, and she was still in the same spot. So, I had sex with her and then went to get help."

The autopsy was the following day. Due to lack of traumatic injury or indication of strangulation, I assumed this would likely be a natural death.

The following day was hectic. Consequently, I could not attend the autopsy. Later in the afternoon, I received a phone call from my forensic pathologist Dr. James Terzian. Dr. T informed me that the autopsy had been completed. He proceeded to explain his findings. He had discovered an enlarged heart, and the cause of death was best described as a lethal arrhythmia.

Dr. T then proceeded to tell me that there was a more detailed cause of death. He replied, "Carb overload," in a calm and sincere voice when I asked what it was.

"Excuse me?" I responded with disbelief.

Now laughing, he said, "I recovered a 3.5 inch in width by 4 inches in length potato measuring 3.5 inches in diameter out of the rectum, hence *Carb overload*."

At the end of the day, the cause was determined to be Lethal Arrhythmia, secondary to Cardiomyopathy, due to the aggravation of the potato and pressure while trying to expel the potato on the toilet. Unsuccessful, she came out of the bathroom, suddenly collapsing to the floor.

I ruled the cause of death as Lethal Arrhythmia and the manner as natural. Needless to say, I did not eat beef stew in my life ever again from that day onwards. Jean laughed.

"Status Quo, Latin, for the mess we're in." This is precisely what I wanted to do, for the time being, to keep things status quo. So, Jean, let's talk about June. "What would you like to know?" she asked. "Tell me about who she was."

Before Jean could answer, a bird flew into the kitchen window, startling us both. Jean quickly spoke out, "Well, maybe I'm next in line to die."

I chuckled. "Tell me about June," I repeated.

"She is a teacher and an artist," Jean replied. "Would you like to see a painting she did?"

"I would love to!" I said, nodding my head.

FIG. 19 JUNE STEVENS PAINTING. PHOTO CREDIT- JEAN STEVENS

"This is a beautiful painting, Jean," I commented.

Going into the living room, Jean suddenly reappeared at the kitchen table. "These are card's that June has made me for all the holidays," Jean said while showing me the cards.

"Wow, Jean. These are really nice," I said.

Jean replied with a gentle smile, "Yes, she has a gift for such things. She also sings. June was once on a ship, and the waves were bad. The ship was rocking. They had June sing to calm everyone down, like on the Titanic."

"They did?" I asked with keen interest. Of course, I had no way of knowing whether this was factual or if Jean was speaking metaphorically.

Jean went on to state, "June will not fly! She won't fly because you're too close to people and you can't breathe! We won't use elevators either!"

"You won't," I replied, chuckling.

"No, no way, none of us will. My mother is the same as her. Would you like to see a picture of my mom, June, and me?" Jean asked.

"Yes, I would."

"Would you like a cookie while I go find a picture?" Jean asked.

"Sure," I replied. Who would turn down a cookie?

Shortly after, Jean came into the kitchen carrying a picture of the three of them. As I looked at the picture, I thought to myself, what a lovely, normal-looking family they were. They were wearing fashionable light-colored dresses in the presence of a rural background. Although this resembles nothing of the June I had been introduced to, I could imagine how fun and loving this family once was.

"We don't like the dark, you know," Jean informed me. "We leave the lights on when we sleep." I didn't pose the question. However, I wondered if she meant June and her in the current times or if she was referring to all three of them.

From a profile perspective, I was starting to get a clearer picture of Claustrophobia, fear of the darkness, and a deep love for her loved ones. Not to mention Jean now is the only one left.

FIG. 20 FROM LEFT TO RIGHT. JUNE STEVENS, BERTHA MATSON, JEAN STEVENS. PHOTO CREDIT- JEAN STEVENS

Jean continued, "We went to the Camptown High School. After graduating in 1936, Jimmy and I traveled the world."

"Oh, that must have been nice."

Jean nodded slightly and continued, "We lived near Pulaski, NY, for a while. I worked in a factory there, and Jimmy was working for General Electric."

"How did you end up with this house, Jean?" I probed. She replied, "Jimmy likes to hunt and fish, so we bought this house. I had the garage built after Jimmy died to keep him in. June and Kemp bought the white house down the road from our aunt and uncle."

"Oh, that beautiful white house just down the road?" I asked as I pointed my finger towards the house.

"Yes, do you want to go see it? Jean asked.

"Yes, absolutely, I would love to," I replied.

Fig. 21 Home owned by June and Kemp currently owned by Jean Stevens. Photo by Thomas M. Carman

"Jean, this house is beautiful. Why don't you live here?" I asked.

"It's too big and needs too much work."

"Jimmy and I moved in here for a while with June and Kemp. This is where my mother came to live when she was diagnosed with tuberculosis. So that is when we moved in," Jean told.

"Well, Jean, I better get you back to your house now. My wife will have dinner waiting soon, so I can't stay here any longer."

"I want you to bring your wife and kids out so I can meet them. Especially your little fellow with Downs," Jean insisted.

"I will sometime, Jean," I promised as I walked back with her. I was getting more comfortable with Jean but taking my wife and kids into an environment where I had just removed bodies is entirely out of the question.

Arriving back at Jean's house, she jumped out and said, "You're going to write a book on me, right? I want you to write a book about all of this," she chirped.

"Jean, I have never written a book," I tried to reason with her.

"Promise me. You will write a book!"

I smiled and said, "I will see you next week Jean."

My ride home was kicking, my favorite artist, *Kiss*, was cranking in the background, and I was reminiscing. Thinking back to my grandmother's house and times with my cousins, sister, and I playing Kiss on her front porch. Not playing Kiss's songs, but we would literally pretend we were Kiss performing in front of a live audience. My sister was the drummer, my cousins were guitarists, and I would sing. We were a crazy bunch of kids, and a few of us still are. Sadly, my only sibling, my younger sister, passed away four years ago from breast cancer. It was a tough time for my family, bringing me to the point where I often thought about my own mortality.

This, in turn, got me thinking back to many of my friends who have left this world, particularly Kerry Lancer. Kerry was a great friend and my go-to buddy. I could always count on Kerry to give it to me straight. He was a regular fixture at my house before moving to South Carolina. Sadly, while in South Carolina, he was killed in a motorcycle accident on April 6, 2000. Kerry had just quit smoking, and the motorcycle was his celebration gift. But unfortunately, that gift took his life. Not a day goes by that I don't think back about the good times he and I had.

Isn't it ironic that we avoid thinking about our own demise yet spend hours thinking back about our loved ones and friends who are no longer here? I've always said everyone wants to go to Heaven, but nobody wants to die.

Chapter 9

GRAM KNOWS BEST, DOESN'T SHE?

A few weeks have gone by now. The weekly meetings with Jean have been educational and exciting, however, I must address the inevitable today. Where are June and Jimmy going? The media has disappeared. Except for Jean and a few neighbors, June and Jimmy have been all but forgotten. Someway and somehow, I need to bring this dramatic event to an end.

Jean meets me at the front door with her usual smiling presence. We sit down, then comes the blunt, blatant question. "When can I have June and Jimmy back?" Jean asks. Weeks of work, and I have essentially gained nothing except insight and Jean wanting a book written on the current affairs of her corpse-collection. "Jean, we need to talk," I replied.

I had her attention almost instantly. "We need to develop a plan of action to have June and Jimmy buried, cremated, or placed in a sealed structure."

"I want them back!" Jean asserts.

"Jean, please, we need to be realistic and legal here," I replied.

"I miss them and want them back," Jean replied firmly.

I asked about June again to change the subject and allowed Jean time to cool off. Then I went on to ask, "Jean, I noticed June had moth balls on and in her. Can you tell me what that was all about?"

"Mothballs do wonders, you know!" Then, with an intrigued look on her face, Jean asks, "How do funeral homes embalm people?"

"Well, it's quite a process."

"What was that plug in June's belly?" Jean asked.

"That's where they put a rod that delivers embalming fluid in the abdominal cavity."

"I like my way better," she replied.

"How is your way better?"

"It was messy dealing with June," I replied. "I tried to keep it beautiful," Jean said.

Sitting with coffee, Jean told me the steps she took to preserve June. "It was difficult getting June out of the ground. The dirt was hard and heavy from being wet. Once we got her on the sofa, I used towels to dry her off. There were bugs, you know."

"I bet there were. What did you do about the bugs?"

"I used nail polish to kill them and keep them away."

"Did that work?" I asked with curiosity.

"Well, it seemed to," she replied. "I washed her hair and combed it, you know."

"I saw that," I replied.

"I used leg cream on her entire body. It kept her nice and tan."

"I wondered how you kept the face so pleasant looking," I replied.

FIG. 22 JUNE STEVENS AGE 66. PHOTO CREDIT- JEAN STEVENS

At this point, I was thinking, *"I can't believe I'm sitting here listening to a woman speak about how she cared for her unearthed sister."*

This reminds me of the time I was at this overdose scene. A man in his late 40's overdosed on Oxycodone. Sitting at the kitchen table were his ex-wife, fiancé, the girlfriend he was cheating on the fiancé with, and his other girlfriend. My friends, you can't make this stuff up! The worse part was that they all knew about each other and were sharing him. Can you imagine? Satan is the master of deceit and lies! Once he knows your weaknesses, it's like sitting at a buffet table with all your favorite foods. Here you can have an *all you can eat service.* Oh, you like sex, here you go!

Jean continued, "I used aluminum foil to keep from seeing into her stomach. Then, I layered potpourri and mothballs on top of the foil. Next, of course, I put her favorite red robe on her to cover everything up. Finally, I put her glasses on her so she could see. She looked so beautiful! I even sprayed her with her favorite Jessica McLintock perfume."

"Yes, I am aware of that. I noticed a nice fragrance, too," I replied. Honestly speaking, I could still smell that perfume in the cooler, along with the putrid odor.

"I gave her sponge baths and brushed her hair daily," Jean went on. "Every night I read the newspaper to her. Then, at 2:30 am, I would go in and kiss her on the cheek so she could sleep peacefully. Then, each morning we would chat about the late evening shows before I would lay down for a few hours to nap. I have a hard time sleeping, you know," Jean said while narrating her experience.

"I remember you were telling me this. How well are you sleeping now?" I asked.

"Terribly, I can't sleep without worrying about June and Jimmy," she replied. "I want June back in the house with me! I will take good care of her," Jean explained. At this point, I realized that Jean wasn't kidding when she said she "Liked June more than Jimmy." Poor Jimmy didn't even get mentioned when Jean mentioned June being back in the house.

"Jean, you do realize that June cannot come back into the house, right?"

"That's just what you keep saying," Jean replied. "Wouldn't it be better to focus on the great memories and put June to rest somewhere?" I tried explaining to her politely.

"I just don't understand why she can't come back here," Jean said in an angry tone.

FIG. 23 RIGHT TO LEFT JEAN STEVENS AND JUNE STEVENS
IN THEIR MIDDLE-AGE YEARS. PHOTO CREDIT- JEAN STEVENS

Then suddenly, Jean changed the topic of our conversation and started asking me about my family. "How is your family?" Jean asked. "Very good," I replied.

"I want you to have something to give to your little fellow," Jean chimed. She was referring to my little son here. Jean came out carrying a small ceramic, multi-colored elephant.

"Oh Jean, that's very sweet of you, but I can't accept this." "Why not?" Jean asked. "It's not professional for me to accept any money or gifts from you."

"Oh, you and your mean laws," Jean replied.

For the most part, I felt terrible for Jean. Many, if not all, think she's a crazy old lady, but after spending so much time with her, I learnt there was more to the whole situation that met the eye. Jean was old with no kids. The only people she was close to and shared her whole life with were her sister and husband. Now one by one, she had to part with both of them. She went through a major change in life without anyone to talk to about it. The causes of Jean's behavior were loneliness and separation anxiety. Adding the claustrophobic piece with my findings would be plausible to label this as a motive. Commonly, a motive revolves around two things: money (a gain or loss of) or love (in love with or fell out of love). To have a case that revolves around only love is refreshing. Although, possessiveness, attention-seeking, and other alternative motives must be eliminated.

The vast majority of homicide and suicide cases investigated revolve around hatred. Hatred for life and health are amongst the greatest of motives. However, there are those cases where suicide occurs on a law enforcement basis. For example, pedophilia with pending charges. Depression or not, such suicide cases create havoc and are highly traumatizing.

Sadly, I know this situation has a negative mental health effect on Jean. Although Jean is always happy to see me, I can feel her disappointment when the back doors of my van remain closed. She anxiously awaits the return of June and Jimmy.

I think we can all share Jean's pain of desperately wanting her dead loved ones back. Let's face it, how many times have we all been disappointed, frustrated, or sick of life? We all differ, but I like to put my faith in Jesus. Noah had a covenant with God. He received the rainbow as a sign that the world would never again be flooded. This is hopeful, but how many are still waiting for their rainbow?

I'm that guy that needs to walk the path seeking out excellence. To a degree, trials and tribulations serve me best. I'm that guy that seems to learn best by knowing burden, pain, and hardship, and seeing it in others allows me to be a light to others. Perhaps I could be labeled as a slow learner. An individual where my thoughts and actions are better left with the Lord. Honestly, we are never closer to God than in times of trouble. I have learned the key is never to allow the problem to come between God and us. Remain focused on God, He will vindicate us from our troubles. We will always come out bigger, stronger, and more faithful.

One of the biggest mistakes we can make is to become entrapped by our troubles instead of reflecting upon the blessings that have previously been bestowed on us. The memories of good things done for us by God become a great fuel for our spiritual fire in times of desperation and aid in fighting the feelings of loneliness, frustration, and helplessness.

Somehow, I need to get Jean to a position of being receptive.

Jean had enough questions for one day and now wanted to hear a story. Since this was the deal between Jean and me, a story must be told. So, I thought carefully about what I wanted to say to her. The story I would narrate to her had to revolve around God. This would perhaps get Jean in the groove and enlighten her to do the right thing the next time we met.

"Jean, I really enjoy attending church each Sunday. It is my time to rejuvenate and prepare for a new week. It took me many years to reach a point of wanting church. But now, attending church is like replacing my old battery with a new, fully charged lithium battery."

Sadly, the church isn't everybody's cup of tea, and I'm smart enough to realize this. But, honestly, for years, it wasn't mine either. All the politics, favored attendees, and the judgment of a few tainted ones made an awful experience for years what should have been a joyful and learning experience."

"Well, people think I'm nuts," Jean complained.

I wasn't a 'born-again' Christian back when Jean and I met or even through our times together. But, looking back, I wish I had been. I could then have told her how the church had a new meaning to me. In fact, many describe a church as just a building. But I would define a church as the body of Christ. A house of repenting and redeeming sinners. Simply put, a gathering for those that desire to give praise and glory to an awesome God who is forever a savior, forgiver, lover, and compassionate living being.

The church I once knew, filled with attitudes and disagreements, is now a house of repenting souls searching for a journey with Christ.

Find a new church if the house of God you attend doesn't feel right. There are many houses of God in the world, and there is one for all of us. Without the body of Christ and all of us within it, a church is just a decorative building.

Fortunately for my family and me, we have found our new home. So, it was a double win. Not only are we surrounded by spirited people, but we are also free from the negatives that once discouraged my family and me from attending church.

"Jean, you know one of the belief systems I've always considered unique is paganism." I joked.

"And who's that?" Jean asked.

"It's an ancient belief system and varies greatly. Paganism has changed a lot from ancient times. It has been greatly influenced by modern belief systems. But most importantly, did you know that modern paganists generally are polytheistic (belief in multiple Gods) or atheists (the idea that there is no God)? Furthermore, did you know that they do not have a Bible or even a set of beliefs to follow?"

"No, I didn't," Jean replied.

"Some may believe in Jesus as one of their Gods, but they do not put any significance in Him. Therefore, a Pagan can't be a Christian. I had a case involving a pagan once."

"Oh wow, it must have been an interesting case to work.," Jean replied.

I went ahead and started telling Jean about the case. "It was a frigid, early February morning. I seriously dislike the weather and often wonder why I don't reside anywhere else than in Pennsylvania. Anyhow, on this early morning, I was contacted by an individual that had entered the emergency department by ambulance. I accepted the case and proceeded to the emergency room.

As I gathered information from the nursing staff and reviewed the EMS chart, I learned that this 31-year-old male had been discovered by firefighters at his residence in cardiac arrest. I would further learn that firefighters had extricated this male from his burning home, carrying him to the front yard where CPR was administered. Ultimately, this male was transported to the emergency department, where his condition remained unchanged. Unfortunately, the emergency room attending physician terminated the resuscitation efforts."

All the while, Jean's eyes remained fully glued to me as I proceeded with my account. She seemed to love my stories.

I continued, "I knew that we were dealing with a fire-related incident at this point in the investigation. Noteworthy to any investigator is that fire is often used to cover up a crime. It takes an incredible amount of heat to burn up human remains completely. Consequently, an accelerant is almost always used when attempting to rid a body by fire."

"What's an accelerant?" Jean asked.

"It's a flammable substance like gasoline," I replied. "How do you know if someone was dead before the fire?" Jean inquired, completely invested in my story.

I went on to explain very superficially how our office handles fire-related deaths. We have protocols followed when investigating any fire-related death at our office. At a minimum, I expect my deputies to perform radiographic and toxicology studies. The omission of radiographic studies makes the investigation susceptible to missing any penetrating or crushing injuries. Either of which could have produced death prior to the fire ignition. If it didn't kill them, it could have contributed to the inability of the victim to escape at the time of the fire."

"Oh yes," Jean replied.

"Equally important are the toxicology studies. It is crucial to discover any illicit or prescribed medications in their system. If present, it is important to question if they played a role in either the death or possibly rendered the individual unconscious, unable to escape the fire. Likewise, sleeping aids, alcohol, narcotics, etc., can significantly alter the ability to awake promptly," I told Jean. "Okay," Jean replied.

A carboxyhemoglobin study is another crucial piece. A carbon monoxide level or lack thereof is critical to our research. This is another tool used to determine whether the victim was dead before or breathing during the fire incident.

Jean then wanted to know if people died from the fire or smoke inhalation. "I have found that most commonly, victims die due to smoke inhalation. Occasionally, we will see a victim that has expired due to an isolated thermal injury, but these are rare" "I see," Jean replied.

"With this pagan case, I proceeded towards the trauma room within the emergency department. Before entering the room, I noted a predominant odor of smoke. This is an odor that I am very accustomed to while investigating a fire-related death. Consequently, there was no doubt in my mind that he was, in fact, in a burning structure. I immediately noted a large framed, 31-year-old male as I opened the door. Not obese, just very tall and big-boned. Under normal circumstances, physical strength should not have played a role in exiting a burning home. However, it is unclear and too early to make that determination. He may have an underlying medical condition that may have limited his ability to escape for all I know.

Looking at the body that lay before me, I notice he is a white adult. His body is positioned supine on a long backboard, commonly found in the presence of cardiac arrest. It is impossible to perform adequate CPR compressions on any form of a cushioned surface due to the softness and inability to compress the heart between the sternum (breast bone) and spine. A backboard is the best approach in the prehospital setting.

Interestingly, the next thing noted before starting my examination was that he was fully dressed, but an oddity caught my eye. Imagine this, Jean, an adult laying in front of you with his shirt up to the nipple line, pants, and underwear down to just above his knees. His genitalia are exposed. Essentially, his knees up to his nipple line were exposed." I narrated the whole view.

"Now mind you, his shirt and wind-style pants were covered with soot as expected. After all, he was inside a burning house. However, the shirt was up, and the pants being down did not make sense."

"How come?" Jean asked.

I told her I wouldn't expect the shirt to be up if his pants came down during rescue efforts. What was really odd was that all his exposed skin was soot-covered, including the genital area.

"Even if his shirt came up and the pants came down during the extrication and/or transport, that would not explain the soot discovered on the exposed area. To me, this could only be interpreted that his pants and underwear were in this position at the time of his death, but why?

I continued my examination of the clothing and external body. Surprisingly, there was no charring on or about the clothing. Nor did I find any charring to the underlying tissue. However, when the shirt was removed, I found superficial burns in a circular pattern to the anterior (front) chest wall. Interesting, how exactly did the man get superficial burns under his shirt without the shirt being burned?

His face presented with both a mustache and beard. The entire face and head are soot-covered. Pupils were brown, and sclera was white. There is no sign of petechiae within the sclera, nor is there yellowing. The conjunctiva present swollen and reddened. Earlobes are bilaterally pierced but otherwise are unremarkable. There is soot noted in the nares and mouth. A good indication that this male was, in fact, alive during the fire and not dead before the fire struck. Teeth were natural, however, in poor condition. I didn't palpate the skull or cervical region due to the radiographical studies that we would perform later.

All clothing was carefully removed, itemized, and cataloged. Then, clothing was placed in evidence bags for further analysis. In full view, the body appears to be externally trauma-free, except for these circular superficial burns of unknown etiology. It was interesting as it seemed.

While examining the pelvis region, pubic hair is present, soot-covered; however, there is no singeing. Genitalia is that of an adult male being circumcised. There are no ulcerations, lesions, or warts within the genitalia region. There is no edema noted in the extremities. Toenails are found to be natural and well-groomed. The fingernails present the same but appear to have dirt or perhaps soot under them. The posterior examination is unremarkable for trauma. There is a posterior livor present with skin blanching in the anticipated regions.

We commonly examine for unique identifiers such as tattoos, piercings, scars, birthmarks, or any other notable findings that could benefit the presumptive identification process. However, in this case, the wife is present in the family room, so positive identification will be made.

While photographing, I did note a large pentagram tattoo on his left upper arm. Additionally, there were other assorted smaller tattoos on his torso. This unique pentagram tattoo would make for an excellent unique identifier had it been needed. Not many in the general population have such a tattoo. For presumptive identification purposes, this would be a great start," I told Jean as she listened intently.

I continued after checking if Jean understood everything up until now. "I just wasn't comfortable with the presentation of soot in the unexposed areas. So, the determination was made to forgo the radiographic and toxicology studies for the moment and plan on a complete autopsy.

Information is now coming in from the scene of this fire. The fire marshal reports that the victim was initially discovered on the property's second floor in what appeared to be a spare empty room.

Photographs revealed a void pattern on the carpet where the victim had laid. When I say void pattern, in this case, I'm referring to the floor being soot-covered, except for the outline where the body had laid. Oddly, the photographs also reveal what appears to be a washcloth near where the victim's head would have been located.

The fire marshal also reports that the actual fire remained contained within the living room. The living room is on the first floor, immediately next to the front entrance door. The fire marshal relayed that his initial findings reflect that the fire's origin was caused by a small electric heater discovered next to the sofa in the living room. She also found the remains of several candles in this same area. The candles would serve as an accelerant to the fire. All of this is excellent information to have while interviewing witnesses."

"Yes, I bet," Jean replied.

"It was fortunate that the victim's wife was in the family room within the hospital. Therefore, contact with the wife would be easy, and we would have privacy during the interview.

Upon contact with the wife, I learned her name is Mary. I introduced myself and expressed my condolences for her loss. Mary was 34 years old. I like to start my interviews by obtaining basic demographical information about the interviewee. This would include full name, including maiden, current address, date of birth, etc.

After receiving this relevant information, I gathered information about the victim. First, basic demographical details of the victim were collected. Then, additionally, I figured what we refer to as victimology data, including educational level, birth location, military service, employment history, friends and/or associates, etc. All of which can assist with the initial profiling of the victim.

Mary was a great historian. I would learn that the victim's name was Ralph. He was a high school graduate, did not attend college, did not serve in the armed forces, was born in Colorado, was right-handed, and was on Social Security Disability for chronic back problems.

After learning these basics, I would move on to the psychological autopsy. Generically this means things that make ralph tick–his hobbies, recreations, addictions, past or current suicidal ideology, actual past suicidal attempts, past incarceration, institutionalization, prior child protective services involvement, etc.

Mary produced very beneficial information for the case. Consider that further details such as additional interviews, research, medical records, and mental health records will be gathered later. Initially, we would get started by gathering any information Mary could provide.

Mary reports Ralph suffers from depression, smokes marijuana, has had a past suicidal ideology, and has past institutionalization. This becomes very important in furthering Ralph's profile.

It's now time for the general interview. Basic questions commonly used to start the discussion would be how long he has been married, whether he has children together or separately, whether there have been any out-of-the-ordinary statements or events recently, whether he has complained of any health concerns lately, and his activities in the last 24 hours.

The past 24 hours of activities could assist in the causation of death and the eventual prosecution of any accused in the presence of a criminal case. The interview would be expanded with additional questions; however, I won't bore you," I said.

"I find this interesting," Jean replied. It was easy to interpret that Jean was an inquisitive person.

"Mary became vague while discussing the past 24 hours of activities. However, she was open, and limited on information provided without being specifically asked a question. This is slightly unusual. Most people being interviewed provide information so quickly that I have difficulty keeping up while documenting.

There is nothing more aggravating than an individual lying to me when questioned. It's like being at an incident where cocaine was the contributor causing a lethal arrhythmia that killed the individual. I ask the witness if drugs were involved, and if they were blatantly lying to me. Like somehow, the cocaine metabolite in their blood will mysteriously disappear when tested. I just want to tap on their head saying, 'Hello, is there anybody in there? The best one, I'm at a suicide scene and I ask the individual present, "Is the gun owned by the decedent?" They reply, "What gun?" "You know, the one that put a hole in your friend's head." Geez, people can be amazingly difficult,' Jean laughs.

"Getting back to Mary. I could interpret this hesitancy as embarrassment, or Mary simply did not want me to know. The last possibility was that Mary was thinking about her responses instead of revealing the straightforward truth.

"Well, what did she say?" Jean asked.

"Mary started out by saying they are both Pagans. Unclear why she started out with this, I posed the question, "Explain that to me?" Mary continues, "We have a polytheistic belief." Mary then proceeded to tell me that Ralph was a homosexual. Thinking I misunderstood her, I replied, "I thought you were married?" "We are, but Ralph is homosexual," Mary answered. "Do you mean bisexual?" "No, he is homosexual," Mary replied. He has a boyfriend he visits, and I have friends who fly from Ohio. We have an open relationship. "So, you have no sexual barriers?" I asked. Mary replies, "That's right."

At this point, I don't know if I'm talking with a suspect or the wife of a man who just untimely died. So, I asked, "What is your occupation? To my surprise, she is a social worker working with troubled youth."

I continued to tell Jean the story, "Throughout the interview, I learned that Ralph had a typical day. He arose this morning and traveled to a nearby town to visit his "friend." When asked to define friend, Mary replied that he was his lover. Then, Mary proceeded, "He returned home in the late afternoon. We had dinner as usual, and the evening course was relatively normal. Later in the evening, Ralph asked if tonight was the night."

"The night for what?" I asked.

"Well," Mary replied.

With this response, now I was curious. I asked what does "Is tonight the night mean?" Mary went on to inform me that they had discussed on multiple occasions a suicide pact. "A suicide pact," I replied. "Yes, we had discussed on multiple occasions about committing suicide together." Intrigued, I asked, "How exactly was this going to occur?" "Ralph has wanted to commit suicide by a fire while having sex." "Excuse me?" I interjected.

Mary continued, "Ralph always had a fantasy about committing suicide by a fire while having sex."

Shocked, I asked, "How did you feel about this?"

Mary replied, "He is nuts, but I knew this when I married him." She went on to say, "When I first met him many years ago, Ralph told me he wanted to die by suicide with fire."

"What did you say to that?" I asked.

Mary replied, "I told him when we get old, and one of us can't function, then we would do it."

"When did the having sex part of it come into play?" I asked.

"Just a few years back," Mary replied.

My mind is working in overload. After all, we are dealing with a fire victim here. Could this have been the night? Did Mary change her mind at the last moment and escape? Did Mary assure that Ralph was dead and then run, not meaning to commit suicide all along? Is it possible that this fire and Ralph's death were totally coincidental? There were so many possibilities at that point. Finally, with great emotion, Jean asked, "What happened?" She was almost like a child waiting for the dramatic ending.

Mary continued, "I usually sleep in the master bedroom alone. Ralph usually sleeps in the living room on the sofa." By talking to the Fire Marshall, I knew that the master bedroom was located immediately next to the living room, with only a door separating the two rooms.

"Do you normally sleep in two different areas?" I asked. "Were there problems with your marriage?" "We had no problems with our marriage," Mary replied. "We occasionally have sex in the bedroom before Ralph goes to the living room to sleep."

"Mary, I need to ask, Was tonight the night?"

"No, in fact, Ralph was furious that I wouldn't agree to it," Mary replied.

"What happened after you told him no?"

"I closed the bedroom door and went to bed," she replied. At this moment, I couldn't help but wonder if Mary was culpable. With this knowledge, should she not have sought professional assistance for Ralph? If she had, would Ralph still be alive?

"Where was Ralph?" I inquired.

"Ralph was on the sofa with several lit candles burning. Ralph loves candles when he sleeps on the sofa. They comfort him," Mary explained.

"Mary, there was a space heater next to the sofa. Can you tell me what that is about?" She explained that Ralph always has a small heater next to the sofa during the cold months.

"We have a big old country house, and it gets cold.", she said.

"Okay. After you went to bed, what happened next?"

"Something woke me up, and I smelled smoke. I quickly got out of bed and opened the bedroom door. I could see flames in the living room."

"Okay, what happened next?" I asked.

"I ran out and yelled for Ralph to get out of the house. He yelled back, 'I will be right out!' So, I ran out the front door and stood in the yard, but Ralph never came out." I noticed that Mary had a couple of teardrops running down her cheek.

"Who called 911?" I asked. "The neighbors. They saw the smoke and fire, I guess," Mary replied. "The next thing I know, emergency responders and equipment started to arrive on location, but still no trace of Ralph."

Mary could not explain why Ralph never came out. She made it clear that he had plenty of time to escape. However, this is what autopsies are for. We will get the answers and fill in the empty blanks."

"I'm curious why he didn't come out?" Jean asked.

"I spent the next 24 hours reviewing past medical history and mental health records. Finally, I met with his psychologist. In the meantime, my colleague in an adjoining county was tracking down neighbors and friends of Ralph to gather additional information," I explained Jean.

"This is interesting," Jean replied.

"Medical records revealed that Ralph had been evaluated and treated for past cigarette burns on his arms. While meeting with the psychologist, I learned that Ralph was a violent man. In addition, he had been incarcerated in Nebraska for child abuse after breaking a 9-year-old's leg. I would also learn that Ralph had been in and out of jail for past drug-related convictions. Jean, this was a troubled man."

"Indeed. He does sound like a terrible man," she replied.

"Medical records also reveal that there has been prior domestic abuse where Ralph was the victim of Mary, leaving Ralph with contusions and lacerations about his torso."

"Really?" Jean asked.

"What I found most helpful was meeting with his psychologist, Dr. Johnson. Ralph had been institutionalized just one year ago. Interestingly, he presented with strong impulses to light fires, hurt himself, and had homicidal tendencies.

Dr. Johnson informed me that on this morning of being admitted, he had spread lighter fluid throughout the residence but didn't light it on fire. Ralph told Dr. Johnson that he found erotic excitement about setting things on fire, and he also had a voice in his head telling him to burn things and people.

Dr. Johnson had diagnosed Ralph with schizophrenia, psychosexual disorder, personality disorder, and depressive disorder with an underlying history of drug abuse and homicidal tendencies. So, a fair question in mind would be, 'Why was Ralph permitted to be in public?'" I told Jean.

"That's a good question," Jean replied.

"Upon completion of the interviews, investigation of records, and autopsy, it was determined that the fire was initiated by Ralph. He had poured hot wax on his chest, leaving the circular burn patterns, bumping the space heater, bringing it in contact with the sofa, and igniting the fire. It was also determined that although the fire was accidental, Ralph decided to remain in the house, go upstairs, masturbate, and ultimately expire due to smoke inhalation.

Evidence revealed Ralph was lying down, masturbating with a towel over his face to endure the smoke for as long as possible before death."

"Oh my!" Jean exclaimed.

As an attempt to make Jean understand, I said, "We are all tempted when lured and enticed by our own desires. Once that desire becomes conceived, sin is born and will bring death upon us as it grows. I'm not referring to literal death. That comes in time. I'm referring to spiritual death. When we experience spiritual death, temptation turns from thought to action, creating sin. Simply put, spontaneous ideas are not what you call sin. Continuous thoughts and scheming and actions are.

Ralph is a great example. Festered by continuous thoughts and desires, Ralph lost the greatest earthly gift, life, combined with spiritual death. To be flawed and empty in heart equates to separation from God.

Chapter 10

FAITH IN JEAN

Hard to imagine it's three days before Halloween, my birthday. June and Jimmy have now been with me for four months and thirteen days. They have had plenty of guests. I continue introducing the cooler's new residents to June and Jimmy as I slide them into their cold resting place. However, I can't imagine if either of them had any idea that this would be where their empty carcasses would be stored.

The last couple of weeks has been both challenging and frustrating. I made a visit to Jean to check in and see where her thought process was, which frankly was unchanged. While researching Pennsylvania Title 28, Health and Safety, Section 1.25 "Disinterment of Dead Human Bodies" subsection D, Exhumation and exposure, I found the following.

The remains of any dead body shall not be exhumed and exposed to view without an order from a court of competent jurisdiction.

Clearly, Jean violated this, and she is fully aware of the violation of this subsection too.

What I really needed was the definition of a structure for deceased remains. I referred to the same document as previously mentioned however this time, I referred to Section 1.22, "Structures for the dead"

(a). Crypt: No dead human body shall be placed in any permanent crypt unless the crypt is fitted with a durable covering that may be tightly sealed after each interment or unless the remains are encased in a sealed container from which no evidence of dissolution may escape.

(b). Mausoleums: No dead human body shall be placed in any; permanent overground mausoleum or other such structure for the dead unless the remains are encased in a container so sealed that no evidence of dissolution may escape. Jean was made aware of this during my last visit.

FIG. 24 MAUSOLEUM, PRICE $108,800.00
PHOTO BY THOMAS M. CARMAN

In the meantime, I reached out to mausoleum distributors to provide Jean with a variety of options. I discovered that these are very out of reach for the average citizen with high-end costs. The least expensive I was able to discover was $108,800.00. This did not include the concrete base or associated labor. Any of the products I looked for would have met the state definition of an acceptable final disposition for human remains. Truthfully, it is highly unlikely that Jean will agree to this product even if she has the funds. Jean was adamant on having them back "As it is." I still have a few tricks up my sleeve in an attempt to outwit the grandma fox.

Hmm, I've been duped. This sounds so much better than deceived or tricked, doesn't it? It would appear that my newly adopted gram had been doing her research since we last met.

Meeting me at the door is Jean with a smirk. In her hand, she has a piece of paper. "Look what I found," Jean said, her eyes glimmering with excitement.

"Jean. This is a body bag."

"You better look again. It is 100 percent heat-sealed and eliminates any possible leakage," Jean continued to explain.

"Jean, this is a body bag designed for transporting bodies, not to permanently be held in," I replied.

"This is what I want you to put them in and then bring them back here!" she exclaimed.

"Jean, I can't do that," I replied.

"But why not?"

Thinking for a minute, knowing darn well I wasn't going to abide by her wishes, I thought I would do a test.

"Jean, we will need to put a lock on the zipper for this to be legal."

"Okay," Jean replied.

"Quickly, and I get to keep the key," I added.

"No, I want the key, I want to be able to open it up, talk to them and bathe them," Jean insisted.

"Jean, this is exactly why this won't work," I replied. She went on to tell that they're 100% sealed and that she's going to order them online. Although I tried my best to convince her not to but knew full well, she was going to.

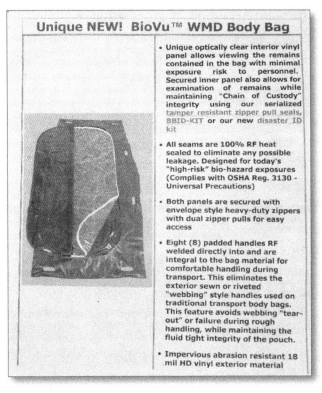

FIG. 25 THE BODY BAG PHOTO BY THOMAS M. CARMAN

After recently speaking with the Area on Aging I was aware that Jean had not been doing very well. She had been prescribed Xanax for her increased anxiety. The separation from June and Jimmy was truly having a negative effect on her. As much as I wanted to help, I couldn't violate the law nor could I overlook the fact that we are dealing with two bodies that are now hazardous remains. So, I was very concerned for the well-being of Jean.

When I asked Jean how she was doing on this visit, she seemed shuffled with her thoughts. Initially, Jean spoke about Ted Bundy.

"I don't know how he escaped," Jean stated. "He killed all those women. Then he didn't want to die, terrible," Jean continued.

"It sure was," I replied.

Suddenly, she went on to talk about the Clintons. "I love listening to Bill Clinton. I think Hillary may be a lesbian," Jean laughingly continued.

Almost in the same breath, Jean reverted to the first day we arrived at her house. "You know, I saw your vehicle with the coroner on it and the cop cars. I thought there was an accident up the road. I couldn't figure out where someone might have died," Jean laughingly stated.

"You never would have guessed we were coming here, huh?"

"No, but I'm glad you did," Jean replied. "I like you, and everyone I talk to speaks highly of you," Jean continued. Something about the latter didn't click, and I started to think if this was sincere or if Jean was being sly.

Jean went on to state, "I don't like people who don't have manners. I've been going to the eye doctors, you know" Jean continued. "I have glaucoma in one eye and edema in the other. I don't want surgery. I'm too old for that."

"Things change when we get older, don't they, Jean?" I asked.

"They sure do," Jean replied. "You know I used to know all the undertakers and went out with them," she continued. "You did? You mean you used to ride in a hearse?" I asked with piqued curiosity.

"Oh yes," Jean replied.

"I can imagine you riding along in a hearse," I joked.

I never was able to confirm if this was the truth. All the old funeral directors and staff were deceased. My fear was that Jean, was starting to slip mentally. I couldn't help but feel that I was playing a role in this day by day.

"How's the family?" Jean asked. "Now, what's his name? Referring to our youngest with downs.

"Terence," I replied. "He was named after my good friend that was killed," I told her.

"Oh, that's nice," Jean replied. "When are you going to bring them out here?" she asked. "I will, Jean," I promise.

"You know my neighbors up above have a son with a speech problem," Jean continued. "They had a speech therapist coming in, and I went to a birthday party the other day, and the boy was speaking."

"That must have been nice."

"Yes, it was."

"Well, Jean, I need to get going. We will be in touch again soon," I told Jean as she hugged me before I left.

I had to get the definition of "sealed" from the Department of Health. I reached out to the Pennsylvania Department of Health. "Yes, sir, I have the bodies of June and Jimmy Stevens. They are the bodies from the Wyalusing area that had been dug up," I told him.

The gentlemen responded, "Oh yes. I remember that incident."

"I still have them at the morgue. Mrs. Stevens is persistent about getting both of them back *as is*. I'm looking for the definition of "sealed" found within your regulations," I asked. "Let me do some digging and get back to you," the gentlemen responded.

I received a call back from DOH stating they can't find anything anywhere. The recommendation was made that I call the solicitor for the DOH in Harrisburg, Pa. Upon doing so, a secretary answered.

"Ma'am, I would like to speak to the solicitor. I need a definition of the word "sealed" found within the regulations of the disposition of human remains."

"Oh, well, she isn't in at this moment. Could I have her get back to you?" the secretary asked.

"Yes, please do,"

After a week, I reached out to the DOH and got offered the same reply. Two weeks later, I attempted again. To this date, I have never heard back from the solicitor. I realized that I was going to be alone on this matter. This was a gray area that, frankly, had not been defined. After all, who would have ever thought that anyone would be digging up their dead family members?

I attended the executive board meeting of the Pennsylvania Coroner's Association. I asked my colleagues, have you ever run into this before? Heads nodded no, and a couple of my colleagues replied, "No," laughing. Our association solicitor was at the meeting. After discussing the case in detail, it was recommended that I file a Declaratory Judgement Action request for the court. The executive board was going to push for legislation defining "sealed container."

I digested what had been recommended on the three-hour ride home with music playing. If I push for a Declaratory Judgement Action, this will bring Jean, a now near 92-year-old woman, in front of the judge. This would bring major news networks back to our county with Jean in the spotlight again. Perhaps she would have enjoyed this, but is this what truly is best for our county or her? Also, let's not forget that Jean will be right back out there, once again unearthing June and Jimmy.

In the absence of a well-defined "sealed" definition from the DOH, I have two choices. First, give June and Jimmy back to Jean and walking away, hoping no one knows the difference, calling it a day, or take Jean in front of a judge. Those are my two choices. I suppose I could just wait it out. No disrespect to Jean but honestly, how many years has she left on this planet? I'll keep June and Jimmy with me and compromise with Jean on the terms. This way, Jean is not breaking the law nor am I. Put us in a gray hole, and we will climb out black and white.

To say I was bitter toward the situation that Jean and I were in would be an understatement. I'm struggling with forcing the court order or protecting Jean from the media circus and judicial system. I may have been a minority when it came to the path I was taking; however, if ultimately a win-win ending came about, who can argue with that? Like I have been told, there's no limit to the amount of good you can do if you don't care who gets the credit.

By now, I have been reading scripture daily, not only seeking answers but for my concern for Jean, her acceptance of death, and, more importantly, her eternity. Admittingly, I wasn't living the way I was scripturally intended to live at the time, but I had faith and belief.

Living in a society where there is always conflict, distortion of truth, egocentric ideology, and a whole lot of bitterness, keeping your faith intact can be challenging. Remembering that bitterness is just self-absorbed anger can be helpful. It's fair to say we all know that one person who is always grumpy with nothing good to say about anything or anyone. Besides being an appalling way to live, it's totally unbecoming to our spirit. The negative effects on our health and spirit have a tremendous impact on our overall health and mental health.

Bitterness is not only toxic to our own being but also to all those around us. After all, who finds joy in hanging out with a hollow person who is always complaining or talking smack about others?

Scripture has taught me this is not God's intent. God wants us to experience peace, hope, love, and happiness (Ecclesiastes 8:15). In fact, if life were one grand, sweet song, I would say start the music. It would appear Jean has become fixated with staring at the album, stumbling away from trust and faith. Perhaps, Jean never had it to begin with. The great news for Jean, no matter how far she traveled off the path of righteousness, God waits with open arms for her return.

Positive vibes and thoughts are essential. If we listen only to society, many would have us believe that those that follow Christ are both intolerant and limited in enjoyment. Society would also have us believe that if something feels good, just do it. When we do, we suffer from the illusion that the behavior is normal and acceptable. This is an illusion, but the consequence is both real and felt. Jean is feeling these consequences as we speak.

We were created to walk with both virtues – faith and personal integrity. Sure, it can be a difficult path; however, we weren't created to walk alone or be alone. We were meant to walk and live with Jesus.

Personal integrity may not bring us an abundance of friends, but it will bring us the right ones. Those that are meant to travel the journey with us. It's better a small serving of vegetables with love than a fattened calf with hatred (Proverbs 15:17). I strive to have true friends who uplift me and avoid those who drag me down. I'm not saying I don't communicate with those that drag me down, and I certainly don't avoid them. I'm saying I'll pet the dog, but I'm not going to sit down and eat out of its bowl.

The following day I received a call from Jean. "Tom, I would like to come out and visit June and Jimmy." she requested. I'll give Jean credit. Her positive thoughts were clear. If she thinks she can, she can in her mind. "Jean, I don't think that is a good idea," I replied. "Well, why not?" she asked.

"We are a working morgue. We are not set up to entertain visitors and have no viewing area. This won't work."

"I'll just come in quick, see them and leave," she replied.

After some convincing, Jean wasn't satisfied but accepted that visiting the morgue would not be an option. Of course, my biggest fear was that she would show up unannounced. Fortunately for me, Jean complied.

Still being in the mindset that I would find a way, I was optimistic that Jean would eventually accept the fact that June and Jimmy's final disposition should be in a legal resting place.

In preparation for my next conversation with Jean, I took the approach of treating Jean as though she is spiritually unaware. If she is in tune with faith, great, but if not, I will be prepared. Either way, I remembered the importance of not judging anyone and prayed that God would use me to change her heart.

The second piece I'm concerned with is Jean's claustrophobic state of mind. This could very well be the main contributor for her actions. Are her claustrophobic fears interfering with her ability to make rational decisions? Questions as such popped in my head.

After learning the victimology of both Jean's mother, Bertha, and twin sister June, it was apparent that Jean's condition was genetic. A genetic predisposition would be logical, with both Bertha and June being claustrophobic.

Knowing that claustrophobia is a fear of being closed in or having no escape, could Jean's position of June and Jimmy be being out in the open ease her fear of the sensation of restriction or suffocation? If Jean connects confinement with danger, she may be hard to convince. If this is her true motive, then I'm left with one course of action. Now I must talk to Jean about faith. Her mind must be opened to the reality of the separation of spirit and soul. June and Jimmy are now empty shells, the remnants of former living human beings.

Chapter 11

FAMILY REUNION

I received a telephone call from Jerry Anderson Contracting. Jerry called to inquire about the design and code requirements for building a crypt on the Jean Stevens property. "I didn't realize that Jean wanted to have a crypt constructed on her property," I replied.

"Yes, she does, and she wants it built as soon as possible," Jerry continued. "Okay," I replied.

"She wants running water in the building, but I don't know how this is going to be possible without a huge expense," Jerry continued.

"Running water?" I asked.

"Yes, she wants running water to bathe them," Jerry explained. "Jerry, you better hold tight until I talk to Jean. She can't bathe them. This structure would have to be sealed with no contact from Jean," I explained.

"Sounds like a plan to me."

On my way to Jean's house, I stopped at a local convenience store for a coffee. While I was there, I ran into one of Jean's neighbors. "What are you up to?" she asked.

"On my way out to visit Jean. She's a pretty stubborn woman." I commented. "She's crazy! I won't take my kids to her house trick or treating. My kids are all scared of her and call her the crazy cat lady," she replied.

At this point, I think for me to consider Jean crazy would be rather presumptuous. I feel that Jean best represents someone who loves dearly, with underlying contributing factors encouraging her rash decisions. Perhaps my delayed indecisive action is promoting her mindset?

I arrived at Jean's house, but this time there was something much different. Jean met me at the door, donning a gray shag wig and thick-rimmed glasses. I must say, she looked strikingly similar to the Austin Powers character. Or let's just say I now have many concerns. Attempting not to smirk, I simply asked, "How are you today, Jean?"

"I'm mad at the contractor," she replied.

I sensed this was not going to be the usual happy visit. When Jean didn't offer me a mug of coffee when I arrived, I knew this was going to be an all-business visit and not our usual pleasant conversational meeting.

"I heard from Jerry inquiring about the crypt. So, you want to put a mausoleum on your property Jean?" I asked.

"Yes. I want it big enough for six people," she continued. "Six people?" I asked, baffled. "Yes, six people," Jean continued. "But why six?" I asked. "I'm not digging yet. Don't worry. This time, I'm getting permits to dig them up."

"Who do you want to dig up?"

"I want my mother, father, Jimmy, June, Kemp since I'm not going to live forever, you know," she replied. "Holy Moly, Jean. You want a family reunion," I replied.

Finally, I got a laugh out of Jean. With a laugh, she replied, "Actually, yes, I do."

Suddenly, Jean offered me a cup of coffee and wanted to hear about how I was doing. I was recovering from surgery at the time. I explained that I was doing fine and recovering as hoped. "Well, how is your family doing?" Jean asked.

"We're all doing good," I replied.

"I can't wait to meet your little guy," Jean continued. "You will at some point," I replied.

"Do people stare or comment on your little one?" Jean curiously asked. "What do you say or do if they do?" she continued.

Thinking about how to respond to Jean's question appropriately, I ran with what seemed natural at the time. "I believe we have an obligation to protect the vulnerable, including the children in this world. I also feel we have an obligation to protect our elderly and those with special needs."

"I believe that too," Jean replied.

"I can assure you that as a parent of a child with Down Syndrome, there are still those that lack understanding and frankly are blinded to the beauty that lies beneath the skin."

"I can imagine," Jean replied.

"A quick trip to the mall, and you soon realize that not all people are accepting of all walks of life. We note the occasional stares and comments. However, predominately, we see smiles and occasional greetings from many while we are at public events."

"That's heartwarming," Jean replies.

"My wife and I attempt to stay involved with special functions in support of children with disabilities. We attend the Special Olympics each year and attempt to make it to the Buddy Walk. When we participate, it's not only for our own son but also for all the kids that are present. Seeing all the support and love there at these events is truly a blessing. The educators, parents, aides, ambulance staff, police staff, and general public supporters in attendance encourage, cheer, and support all the children. The love and smiles from the athletes themselves are just priceless." "Oh, how nice this is," exclaimed Jean.

"Jean, did you know Jesus Himself took a child from the crowd and said, "Whoever welcomes one of these little children in my name welcomes me, and whoever welcomes me does not welcome me but the one who sent me" (Mark 9:36-37)?

Jean nodded, conveying that she had heard of that verse.

"Personally, I love this, Jean! God loves all His children, and regardless of our age, we are all His children. In fact, God instructs us to be like children. We are to come to Him full of faith and trust." I spoke.

I could tell by the expression on Jean's face she may not be sold on this. "Well, in my day, if you misbehaved, you got the belt, hose, or switch," Jean replied.

"Well, I never got whipped with one of those items, but the yardstick was my mother's tool of choice. I can't begin to tell you how many times my mother would crack me with a yardstick. The funny part was that she broke several of them while smacking me, which of course, would just anger her further." Jean laughed as I narrated the telltales of my childhood.

"Let me tell you when I was in high school, the principal would give me a crack with "Big Bertha," this was a thick wooden paddle. Now, this would get your attention," I said.

"I bet," Jean replied.

"Here's the thing, Jean, we are instructed in scripture to love, discipline, and teach our children. However, this can be difficult in today's world. In fact, mundane moments can be challenging and frustrating." I continued to speak. "How so?" Jean inquired.

I told her that sometimes, for example, when I let my guard down at the mall and notice someone staring at my son, I have the desire to lash out.

"On multiple occasions, I wanted to get in someone's face and pose the question, "What are you staring at?" However, scripture tells us to be alert and prepared for such moments. I have to see it for what it is, spiritual warfare, and guard my heart. When I have these moments of weakness, I must remember we do not live for our own glory but for the glory of God. We must ask, what would Jesus do?

Sure, I wanted to plow someone in the face but is this what Jesus would do? "It's ridiculous that someone would stare and be rude," Jean replied.

"It sure is, but it is what it is," I replied.

"I firmly believe that children are a gift from God. Any gift from God comes with both knowledge and love. In my home, we have an open communication policy. We have always spoken with our kiddos at an early age about the trials in life and errors, including addiction, suicide, etc. We have also been open in asking about bullying. Have they bullied any other kid, or are they themselves being bullied? If they have been bullied, we ask, how did this make you feel? Giving them every opportunity to talk to us about it openly."

"That's good," Jean replied.

"Our goal as parents is not to win an argument but win the soul by leading them to Christ. Jean, it's tough with our current culture. It's difficult as a parent to direct our children in the right direction when we're up against social media and loose rules and ideology. Honestly, it becomes very complicated with so much vulnerability and promotion of whatever makes you feel good mentality. It's not like when we were kids anymore. Cammy and I had to adjust and learn this. You have to be much more creative with raising kids in this age. 'Do as I say and not as I do' does not work with modern-age kids. The frustrating part is balancing our ideology with God's ideology," I further elaborated.

"What do you mean?" Jean asked.

"I can be stubborn at times, Jean. I tend to get involved and authoritative at times with the kids because, frankly, it's easier! It's my way or the highway! The complication is that this can lead to a disconnect between the love of Jesus and my own behavior. Cammy and I tend to want to attack the behavior. This would work for younger kids but leads to a brick wall barrier with our older kids. Youth are learning more in a quicker amount of time than when we were young. We didn't have internet and cell phones when we were kids."

"We sure didn't," Jean replied.

"What Cammy and I really want to do is get to the root of the problem. We can only do this if we let the Holy Spirit in and accept what it teaches and not our own understanding. Let's be honest here; children are experts in dividing and manipulating Mom and Dad to get what they want. If Mom says no so, they will go ask Dad or vice versa. We have found that my wife and I must be on the same page. This means we must communicate before having a knee-jerk reaction with one of the kids. Our practice is to discuss what is best for our child."

"Sounds about right," Jean replied.

"Cammy and I try to think about what Jesus would inspire us to do? What is our role, and what role, if any, can our fellow Christians play in assisting us during times of trouble? Praise God, we have never had any of our kids suffer from addiction, but if we had, this would be an example of when we might reach out to our Christian friends.

Another thing that we have learned is that sometimes a child must experience the ramification of their poor choice. It may be painful for Cammy and me, but for us to enable them serves no value. Fighting the battle personally, with the help of God, scripture and our input as parents, often leads to a better result.

For example, if one of our kids gets mad and throws their video game remote, and it breaks, well, guess what? We're not going to run out and replace it with a new one. Instead, they need to learn that this was inappropriate behavior that comes with a consequence. As parents, we must tell them why this behavior is inappropriate. It's even more productive when we back it up with scripture."

"Oh," Jean replied while taking a keen interest in the conversation.

"Jean, I was always taught what a child hears and sees today; they imitate later in life. If Cammy and I start them off on the way they should go, even if they get off the path, they more than likely will return to their faith.

Jean, imagine how good life would be if everyone held on to the promises of scripture and abided by the commandments. Homicides would be at an all-time low. Rape would be a rarity, and drug overdoses would be nearly non-existent. The quality of life would improve if only we all chose to believe in something greater than ourselves.

"Possibly," Jean said. I saw her contemplating before asking the next question, so I waited.

"Do you ever have any cases involving kids?" Jean asked while looking at me. She judged by my expression and looked down. "I don't know how you do it," Jean continued.

"I do, and it is never easy. I will be completely honest with you. There are times that, even as a Christian, I find myself confused about the death of a child. Why is the life of a child taken? It's unnatural for a parent to have to bury a child! No case has a greater emotional effect on me, yet I continue to have deaths involving children year after year.

"Do you ever think about your kids when you have a case involving a child?" Jean asked.

"There was one case that deeply affected me in a way that I have never experienced before," I replied.

"What was it about?" Jean asked.

"I recall one specific case that would test my vulnerability and emotional connection to the maximum. It was a case where I would find myself, for the first time, so temporarily distraught that I would actually have to excuse myself from the examination on three separate occasions throughout the examination.

"Although this had never happened to me before and hasn't happened since, it was a scenario that disrupted my mental resolve without mercy. Actually, on three separate occasions, while performing my duties, I was momentarily numb, with my performance being temporarily halted," I replied.

"Really?" Jean replied as she looked dismayed.

I was contacted directly and informed that a medical helicopter was inbound with a pediatric cardiac arrest. This was rare. Normally a cardiac arrest is taken by ground and not by air. However, maybe the child went into cardiac arrest while being airlifted to the hospital.

Upon my arrival at the hospital, a friend of mine who was one of the flight attendants informed me that this child was removed from the scene in traumatic cardiac arrest solely due to the dynamics and mental health of the surviving family members who were at the scene.

This is a scenario that I can certainly relate to after spending many years in the prehospital arena and being in that same position. Prehospital determinations are not always easy and, frankly are determined on a case-by-case basis. In those remote times, transporting an obvious dead child dominates doing nothing. This is a judgment call, and its conclusion determines pronouncing or transporting. Upon being made aware of the scenario, this would certainly be one of those judgment calls that I agreed with.

As I made my way to the trauma bay, walking down the hall, I noted a few nurses with tears in their eyes. This is a somber reminder of a child's death's emotional effect on healthcare workers. God bless all our nurses throughout this country. Very few people realize the emotional roller coaster these nurses endure. From the barking out directives physicians order, and bedside manner expectations, to the trauma and medical illness seen. They absorb it all in the name of nursing.

With the trauma bay door in view, I noticed the blinds closed and the inner room darkness. There were bloody footprints about the entryway, secondary from the feet of all who attempted to help. Upon opening the trauma bay door, I noted what appeared to be a male who was obviously very young. I turned the overhead lights on. Making my way to the bed, I noted a small physique. The sheet covering him was blood-soaked, and there was blood on the floor. Multiple IV bags and blood were at the bedside. IV catheters were located in both venous and arterial sites. An endotracheal tube was inserted into the mouth and advanced into the trachea. Cardiac monitor leads and defibrillation pads were strategically located about the torso. The cardiac monitor remained on and revealed a flat line known as asystole.

Looking at his face, hair, eyes, and facial features, it suddenly struck me that he looked just like my son Dominic. The resemblance was uncanny. In my mind, this young man looked exactly how my son would look in just a few years. In fact, everything about this boy resembled my son. From the height, weight, eye color, and hair color, all strikingly resembled my son.

Overwhelmed with emotion, I suddenly had to exit the room and go out of sight down the hallway. While standing in the hallway, I found myself coming to tears. This has never previously happened while performing my duties. Sure, on the way home, I jam to music and occasionally shed tears but never have I had to exit a room.

After a few minutes, I returned to the trauma bay to initiate my examination and fact-finding. While pulling down the blood-stained sheet covering his small framed body, I noted a large, 6cm in diameter, gaping hole in the left side of his chest. The wound was on the lateral chest wall. Within the opening, I noted the remnants of the myocardium (heart). I also had a plain view of a significantly damaged lung.

For the second time, I found myself leaving the room. I just could not shake the vision of someone like my son lying there. I'm not sure what was worse, the vision of my son or the embarrassment of leaving the room again. This was something the nurses were not accustomed to seeing me do.

I returned to the room to get my act together for the second time. Continuing the examination, I noted no other trauma to the torso of this child. Anatomically speaking, he presented like you would expect any other 10-year-old to present.

I abruptly halted my exam as I heard a knock on the trauma bay door. Answering, "Come in," the clinical coordinator presented.

"Tom, the father and brother of this boy, just arrived with the police. Is it okay if I bring them in?"

I replied, "Let me meet with the investigator first to get some background on this incident."

The officer and I went to a private area within the hospital. After posing the question, "What happened?" The officer stated, "It's an unfortunate situation. The father and the two boys live alone. The mother is out of the picture."

"Oh, is he widowed?" I asked.

"No, the mother was involved in drugs and abandoned them. She is out west into prostitution, according to law enforcement in the town she now lives. The boys both have significant learning disabilities. The father, as you will see, also has some disability. The father went out hunting this morning, leaving both boys at the house. When he left, he forgot to lock the gun cabinet, leaving several loaded weapons in the cabinet. The home is a two-story dwelling with a full basement, where the gun cabinet is located."

"So, the guns were all loaded?" I asked.

"Unfortunately, yes."

The boys normally go to school and participate in a special program for their disabilities. However, today, they stayed home. The boys went down into the basement and retrieved two shotguns. As they were playing, what the surviving child said, cowboys and Indians, they would run between the basement and first level. The surviving child was in the basement hiding when the decedent came down the stairwell. As the decedent was coming down the steps, the brother pointed and pulled the trigger. Scene findings confirmed the trajectory, and blood spray, droplets, and splatter confirmed the same.

After obtaining information about the weapon, I learned that this was a 12-gauge shotgun loaded with buckshot that the surviving child used. With this being a distant shot, the gaping wound in the chest of the 10-year-old would make sense. After clarification from the police agency involved, I determined that the manner of death would be accidental versus homicide. Since the scene was in an adjoining State, I would rely heavily upon that jurisdictional law enforcement for scene evidence and their interpretation."

"Oh, I see," Jean replied. "I wondered how that worked," Jean continued.

After discussing the case with the police, I returned to the trauma bay. Upon returning, I nodded to the clinical coordinator, meaning she could now bring the father and surviving son into the room. As the clinical coordinator exited the room again, I had to step out of the room to compose myself.

Upon re-entry into the room, the door suddenly and slowly started opening. The hospital clergy followed by the father and the surviving son were in the lead. Standing before me was a tall, thin, and fragile man. His hair was dark brown and curly. I noticed both ears had large hearing aids. He was wearing an insulated camo jacket with a blue tee-shirt underneath. He had on blue Jeans that showed wear. On his feet were a pair of white sneakers. I noted a blood smear around his sneakers and on the sleeve of his jacket, presumably from his deceased 10-year-old son.

Following the father was the other son. The boy presented in a tee shirt and pajama bottoms. He had sneakers on his feet. The boy had dark brown straight hair that slightly covered the tips of his ears. His eyes were brown, resembling his deceased brother in stature. I noted dried blood on the hands, presumably from attempting to assist his now-deceased brother after accidentally shooting him.

I slowly approached the father, named Timothy. I placed my hand on his left shoulder as I offered condolences for his loss. He nodded, acknowledging my condolences. I then turned to the young boy and put my hand on his left shoulder. The boy named Ralph was crying and scared. My heart was breaking for them both.

In a loud voice, Timothy asked if he could see his son. His speech pattern was both mumbled and difficult to understand. Later, I would find out that he usually engages in sign language. I shook my head yes in approval of Timothy seeing his son. Timothy approached his son and placed his hand on his bloody forehead. Tears were streaming down Timothy's cheeks. Ralph stood close by the side of his father at the bedside.

There was great concern for the father. The consensus was that he was at great risk for self-harm. This was felt by all parties involved. Statements that were made were, "It's my fault," "I should be dead," and "I don't want to live anymore." These statements directly result from feeling responsible, guilty, fearful, heartache, and hopeless. My feelings I did not share. I know in my heart there is supernatural strength and healing when you claim the power of God. The thief comes only to steal and kill and destroy; I have come that they may have life, and have it to the full (John 10:10).

This assures me that this child's death is from the evil one, not God! This also assures me that this child now has life in fullness with Jesus. However, this is not something I was going to share with a man who just lost his son."

"I don't blame you," Jean replied. "People don't want to hear about God when they just lost someone they love," Jean continued.

"Well, Jean, I have to get going. We will talk again in a week or two." I told Jean.

"Sounds good to me," Jean replied. Unfortunately, my ride home was somber that night. Rehashing this story to Jean brought back a lot of memories that I had strategically filed in the back of my mind. I struggled with selecting a musical genre; everything just worsened my mojo. So, I drove in silence, attempting to break the funk I was in.

Chapter 12

HARDBALL 101

I had just returned to the morgue from an incident. An incident I won't soon forget. I had received a call advising me of a death at a private residence. The information provided led me to believe this was a natural death.

Upon arriving on location, I was greeted by Paul LaFrance, lead investigator with the state police. "I hope you brought your muscles with you," Paul joked.

"A large person?" I asked.

"You could say that," Paul replied.

The home was a single-story, ranch-style home. Upon entering the residence, the interior in view was orderly and intact. Other than layers of dust covering all surfaces, the residence was pristine. Continuing through the residence it would appear that the property had not been occupied in quite some time. Making our way to the rear of the property, the bathroom is noted to be dirty and untidy. It would appear that the bathroom was a catchall for assorted items. Immediately after the bathroom was a bedroom.

This is where it became very interesting in a morbid sort of way. Frankly, I couldn't believe what was before my eyes. Imagine, 24 inches in depth, diet soda 2- liter soda bottles on the entire floor surface. On top of the bottles lay the body of a male. The male presented with long, gray, dirty wavy hair. His hair was matted. On his face was an untrimmed gray beard. It also was matted, crusted with grime. The male was wearing a dirty tee shirt and a pair of dirty shorts. His legs were the size of my chest in diameter. The skin presented with what most likely was Ichthyosis. Scaly, dry, peeling, and weeping.

Imagine being imprisoned in a single room, being so large that it is impossible to exit through a doorway. This male weighed 800 plus pounds. Tragically, this male sat and slept on a mountain of empty 2-liter soda bottles. His diet consisted of bread, canned soup, and unrefrigerated lunch meat. Later learning that a friend would deliver these items to him weekly through a window in the room of entrapment.

There were no clothes in the room other than that of which this male was wearing. A large pail was present, used for urinating and defecation. On the pile of bottles in a corner was an electric hot plate for warming his soup in a small pan that had not been washed in years. Empty soup cans were piled in an adjoining corner.

After photographing and assuring this was a natural death, the process of planning the removal came into play. This was the difficult part. We would not be able to bring him through the doorway, nor would he fit on a stretcher. In addition, we're talking about a man who won't fit in a conventional transport van.

It was concluded that the local fire department would be contacted. The fire service is accustomed to extricating and would certainly have any tools that would be required for the job.

Upon the arrival of fire officers, collectively, we discussed the situation and complications. A decision was made. The only safe way to remove the decedent was to expand an existing window. The fire chief made the executive decision to expand the window by utilizing a chainsaw. This would make a larger opening in the bedroom wall, essentially making a larger window.

Now that a plan was in play for a larger opening, the task of how to physically get the decedent up and out of the room was discussed. Obviously, conventional methods were not going to be applicable; therefore, the decision was made to use a large tarp.

This would require many strong arms, and we now have several firefighters on the scene. The sawing then began. Once completed, the tarp was brought in. I learned many years ago how insightful and helpful our local firemen are. My standard practice is to stay out of their way. However, I cannot begin to express the gratitude I have for these folks.

Once the firemen had the decedent placed on and secured within the tarp, it was now time to exit. It took ten firefighters to lift and carry the decedent. He was out of the residence, but what do we do with him now?

Dignity and grace are a huge part of our office. However, occasionally we are left with tough decisions. This was one of those moments. After careful consideration, the decedent was placed into the back of a pickup for transport. Once completed, imagine the bed of a pickup completely filled with a man. This is what we had.

While transporting him to the funeral home, a call was made to prewarn them of our situation that was soon to be their situation. We were aware of how unloading the decedent would be challenging. Upon arriving, a backhoe and large straps were waiting. Again, far from the norm, thinking outside the box was necessary.

The decedent was strapped and lifted out of the back of the truck and then lowered onto a large platform. At this point, the coroner's office is released from responsibility, other than the normal investigative and paperwork.

I couldn't help but feel bad for the funeral home. With decedents of this size, cremation becomes a concern. Morbidly obese individuals will not fit in a regular cremation furnace, making it necessary to deliver them out of the area to a facility that can handle individuals of this size. There's an elevated risk with cremation due to size, tissue, and extreme fat. All of these can produce extremely high heat combustion and increase fire risk within the furnace and chimney.

Arriving back at the morgue, a phone message was waiting for me from Jerry, the contractor. I returned to Jerry's call.

"Tom, I wanted to let you know the concrete slab has been completed for Jean's crypt."

"Okay," I replied.

"Jean has provided me with quite a list of things she wants in the crypt that I wanted to talk to you about," Jerry continued.

At this point, I could only imagine what Jean had in mind. "What does she have in mind?" I asked out of curiosity.

"Well, she wants a cement floor, bright overhead lights, cement block walls, two overhead heaters, four vents in the wall near the floor, a metal ceiling, a steel entrance door with PVC frame, double-locking doors, a sink with running water, tables 30" high and 80" long with mattresses and vinyl siding on the outside," Jerry replied.

"Oh, and she wants a security system with a siren installed," Jerry continued.

"My God! Jerry, I know you are in a bad spot but taking Jean's money on this project when I know those bodies aren't going to be in this structure seems unfair," I continued.

"I know, but what else am I supposed to do? She has the money and is demanding that I build this crypt."

"I will be speaking with Jean tomorrow and find out where she's at with things," I replied.

Upon arriving at Jean's home, I noted the concrete slab across the road.

Fig. 26 Concrete slab for the crypt.
Photo by Thomas M. Carman

Jean came sprinting out of the house and met me by the van. "What do you think?" she asked. "It looks pretty nice," I replied. "I have a question, though. That list you provided Jerry is pretty intense. Why will you need all that stuff inside the crypt?" I continued. "Well, I'm going to need it, you know," Jean replied.

My phone suddenly rings. It is the 911 center, and I have a motor vehicle accident I need to respond to. "I have to go. I will try and get back out tomorrow." I told her, and she replied with a nod.

Tomorrow turned into a couple of weeks due to the office being busy. When I did return to Jean's, she was now 92 years old. She had a birthday a few days ago. When I went back to Jean's, I saw something that shocked me. A fully erected structure that looked no more like a crypt than a food vending truck. It was a stick-built structure with vinyl siding. I immediately noticed a white insulated household door. This was a problem! It was time to have a heart-to-heart with Jean, and I knew she would not like what I had to say.

Once again, Jean came sprinting out to meet me by the van. I just can't believe how agile this 92-year-old friend of mine remains. Upon meeting me, she immediately states, "Let's go inside," meaning inside her definition of a crypt. Jean opened the door, and I followed her in.

FIG. 27 BUILDING THAT WAS ERECTED FOR THE PURPOSE OF A CRYPT.
PHOTO BY THOMAS M. CARMAN

All things except the sink and running water that Jerry had informed me about were, in fact, in place. It looked like a social house for the dead, including above-head heaters to keep all parties warm.

Good God, it looked like a mass casualty portable operating room inside. The tables had a 2" thick mattress on each table. They were ruggedly constructed and could easily bear the weight of a human body, even one that had been dead and decayed for months and years. The concrete floor had even been finished and polished. Although it was one elegant castle for the dead, the reality is, this cannot happen unless the door is permanently sealed.

FIG. 28 INSIDE THE CRYPT. PHOTO BY THOMAS M. CARMAN

"Jean, we need to discuss the door," I said. "What about it," Jean replied. "I have to be assured that this door will be permanently sealed," I told her. "No problem, I'm going to have it doubled locked," Jean replied. "I will be the only one going in," she continued. "I'll bathe them, read to them, and drink my coffee with them," she continued. "Jean, here lies the problem," I began to explain. "You cannot continue to do what you have historically done," I said blatantly.

This was a difficult conversation to have with a woman that I now viewed as a grandma figure. I knew in my mind that this would either go well or potentially end our friendship and ongoing communication.

"I don't understand what the big deal is," Jean stated. "They used to lay the bodies out in parlors at people's homes for days awaiting the arrival of out-of-town relatives. People would come in and eat with the body in the home," she continued. "This may be true, Jean, but the bodies were not left out permanently, as you propose to do."

"Jean, you know I care for you, and you also know that I view you as a grandma figure to me. However, this must come to an end! We have three choices, Jean. The first is that June and Jimmy can be placed in a legal final disposition container as a casket and vault, placed as a green burial, cremated, or placed in a sealed mausoleum. The second choice, a court order, is obtained to do the previously mentioned steps. The third choice we leave June and Jimmy where they are until you take your last breath. These are our choices!"

Jean remained silent for a few moments, then stated, "I have two lawyers, you know?" "I know, but are you prepared to make a debacle out of this?" I asked. "If you seek legal counsel with the expectation of getting June and Jimmy back to your home, two things will occur. One, it will be a media circus bringing unnecessary attention to you, to me, and the county. Second choice – the Judge will ultimately order June and Jimmy to be placed in a sealed and secured container. Guaranteed Jean! I only say this because I care about you."

"I don't care," Jean replied. "I want them back!" she remained adamant on her stance.

My words appeared to have a profound emotional impact on Jean. With the realization and a collective sense that all this time invested was with negative achievement and of no good.

Concerned, I spoke to Jean. "Sometimes, things fall apart, so better things can happen. I know you have love, fear, compassion, and temptation."

I realize the temptation is real and often in our faces. But I also personally believe this is not by chance but by and from the spiritual warfare that is present on Earth.

Honestly, temptation comes in pretty attractive packages. To you, June and Jimmy in your house sound logical, but we must remember that evil makes things look good and logical. After all, he is the master liar who is full of deception and untruth.

I'll be honest with you, Jean. My daily temptations include booze, gambling, fast times, and sexual immorality. I'm not going to stand here and blow smoke up your butt. We're all in this together, Jean. We are sinners! However, Jesus died, was buried, resurrected, and paid the ultimate price for our sin with His blood.

Jean sat quietly, taking it all in. I stood up, intending to ask the question that needed to be asked. This question is not a question I would ever ask on a death scene. However, I'm here as a friend and not as the Bradford County Coroner at the moment. My standard practice is not to mention God unless a family does first. If so, then I will participate in an open dialogue with the family.

Well, here it goes! "Jean, I'm worried about you." "Why?" Jean asked.

"Jean, you're now 92. Are you prepared to die? More important-ly, do you believe in God?" I asked her.

Jean thought for a moment and then replied, "I don't go to church all the time, but I go once in a while. I'm not a heathen, you know?"

"I know, Jean, but do you believe in Jesus?" I asked.

Avoiding the question, Jean replied, "I question the Bible and its authenticity. I believe there is something out there; somebody creat-ed our eyes and minds, you know? I don't know about the afterlife. You know, most people believe when you die, that's it! If everyone believed this, there wouldn't be all these religions. Every 20 years, there are wars, you know," Jean continued.

I must say, Jean put an interesting spin on my question without directly answering the question. She should have been a politician! I know from experience how Satan works. He tempts us by shooting random thoughts into our minds. God protects us by giving us the ability to process and recognize this as temptation. Sin is not in the thought but in acting upon it. Simply put, we can't help what comes into our thoughts, but we can help how we react to them. This has to be my goal with Jean. Get her to accept Jesus and release this temp-tation to physically possess June and Jimmy.

"I'm a doubting Thomas, you know," Jean continued. All these religions, the Jehovah's Witness people, come to my house with their magazines. I let them talk. It gives me something to do. I love missionary preaching," Jean stated. "You do? Why's that, though?" I asked. "I think it is nice that people go to other countries and try to help people." "Sometimes we need encouragement in life. Who better to encourage than fellow brothers and sisters in Christ," I replied. Jean smiled.

Wanting to encourage Jean and plant a few more seeds for her consideration in accepting faith, I continued.

"You know, Jean. I feel many don't seek and accept faith due to convincing themselves they are not worthy. Somehow, they feel they are an oddity that is not worthy of the love of our Lord. This isn't true. This is just another lie from the evil one. As far as temptation, Jesus was tempted in every way by the evil one. Why would we think we're any better?" "I'm listening," Jean interjected.

At this point, I seemed to have Jean's full attention, and I didn't want to lose it. So, I continued, "Many don't have or won't admit they have faith. This isn't good. If someone denies Him, He will deny them. Many are too concerned with trying to impress others. Not only is this energy and time lost, but think about it; we all know someone who tries to impress you with their money, education, experience, or a host of other things. I call them one-uppers. You try to tell them something, and they interrupt you because they have done something better. Egocentrism at its finest! The moment we stop trying to impress others is the very moment we will experience a sense of freedom and excel with positive energy."

"Those are the type of people I don't care for," Jean interjected.

"Jean, the sooner we stop trying to control things and people, the happier we will become. We're kidding ourselves if we think we have ever been in control. The sooner we realize this, the sooner we will be on the path of righteousness. Don't get me wrong here. We have control by free will to do whatever we want. We can dance with demons, or we can dance with angels. Dancing with angels may not result in all the happiness or fun, but it will give you peace! Dancing with devils may give you momentary or temporary happiness, but it will not give you long-lasting eternal peace." "I love listening to you talk about this," Jean interjected.

"We can have fun as Christians, Jean. In fact, Jesus wants us to have fun and be happy. He's not an authoritarian or dictator. He just wants us to experience happiness and be healthy, and it's our choice; we have free will," I continued.

There are two spiritual forces in this world. The first is a good spirit that is Christ-filled. The second is a bad spirit that is evil-filled. They fight daily, unseen, trying to win our souls. The spirit is the most important part of our existence. It influences our soul, which influences our hearts and actions.

"Jean, imagine us being an egg. Now, imagine the shell as our body (brain and heart), the yolk as our soul, and the egg white as the spirit. The spirit (good or bad) influences our yolk, which in turn influences our shell (heart and brain). But if we crack the egg, our shell is broken, but our yolk and egg white remain. By spiritually feeding our soul and shell, not only will we find peace, but when we die, the shell is left alone here while our yolk and egg white move on to eternity. Based upon whether our soul was good or bad dictates our final destination, Heaven or hell. Bringing new meaning to whether we are a good or bad egg." "You're funny," Jean chuckled.

"So, how do you know Jesus is real?" Jean asked. "I don't, but I have faith," I replied. "Do you go to church?" Jean asked. "I do, but I'm not saying you must attend church to have a personal relationship with Jesus. What I am saying is that it is easier to be surrounded by fellow believers than to attempt to walk the journey alone."

"For where two or three are gathered together in my name, there am I in the midst of them." (Matthew 18:20). "Jesus desires to have a personal relationship with each of us." "Okay, but how do you know this is real?" Jean asked.

I've always respected this question and feel it is a fair question that deserves a fair answer. "So, Jean, you're asking me why I'm a Christian, correct?" "Yes!" Jean responded.

"Well, my mind works in an investigative fashion. After all, investigating and profiling is my career. With this in mind, things need to be both logical and factual for me to draw a personal conclusion.

Let's talk about logic and facts. As you know, a body doesn't have to be present to pursue a homicide charge, nor does a body need to be present to obtain a guilty conviction.

When we present key pieces of evidence and factual testimony based upon a reasonable degree of scientific and/or medical certainty that a homicide has occurred and the accused had motive, opportunity, and performed the act. This produces logic and fact beyond a shadow of a doubt without a physical body present.

"Now, let's apply this to faith. The fact that Jesus has not been physically seen in over 2,000 years here on Earth doesn't equate to Him not existing.

With the production of physical and testimonial evidence, faith becomes more realistic. At the end of the day, accepting Christ still remains an act of faith. If we could physically see Jesus, it wouldn't be called faith now, would it? However, faith is exactly what's required to be a spirit-filled Christian."

"True," Jean replied.

"Let's start with evidence, Jean. Out of all the belief systems in the world, only Christianity is deeply planted in history and evidence. Unlike other belief systems, Christianity reflects the reality of our present existence. Look around Jean; everything that's happening in the world has been prophesized within scripture. No other belief system has this," I told Jean.

Additionally, archeology evidence throughout the years supports writings found in scripture. Archeologists continue to discover more solid evidence that supports the writings and teachings of the Disciples. In other words, there is archeology evidence that validates the New Testament. From the Ark of Noah to the discovery of the ancient tomb where it is believed Jesus was laid, buried, and resurrected, archeology has contributed to the validation process, leaving the faith as the last validation. As absolute truth, no other belief system can offer archeology evidence that would support their belief.

Now I want to share with you some miracle evidence. I think everyone finds joy in hearing about modern-day miracles. Undoubtedly, there's something about miracles that pull at our heartstrings. Is this coincidental? I think not. We were created to recognize these miracles and give praise and thanks.

I'm going to share with you a personal miracle that I experienced. At the age of 25, I required a pacemaker for a condition called Sick Sinus Syndrome. I had a lazy sinus node (natural pacemaker). It was lazy and would cause my heart rate to decrease to a life-threatening low rate, a condition called bradycardia. The etiology was determined to be alcohol-related cardiomyopathy.

I would have a permanent pacemaker for years to come. With time I would need to have several pacemaker (generator) replacements. This was a simple procedure that was generally a same-day surgical intervention. I would be medicated, bandaged, and sent on my way.

Initially, I would have to call the arrhythmia center every six months for my pacer activity to be read over the phone. As technology advanced, I would have a device next to my bed to interpret my pacer activity and submit the data directly to the arrhythmia center as I slept.

When you have a pacemaker, there are two things that you absolutely do not want. You do not want an eroded pocket. Generically speaking, you do not want the pocket to open up. Secondly, you do not want an infection in or around the pacemaker site. Both of these can come with a high risk of mortality, especially the latter.

One evening as I lay on the sofa, I looked down, noticing my pacer site was reddened and sore. Thinking that I somehow irritated it during physical exertion or sleeping, I made a phone call to discuss it with my cardiologist.

An appointment was made with my cardiologist. The appointment went well, with oral and topical antibiotics being initiated. After a few days, the redness cleared up, and all was good, or at least I thought.

Several days later, in the afternoon, I noticed a stain on my shirt in the area where my pacer was implanted. Upon lifting my shirt and inspecting the site, I saw an opening in the corner of the pacer pocket oozing a discolored fluid.

Having an understanding that this was a very bad sign, Cammy immediately took me to the emergency department at the facility where my cardiologist was located. To no surprise, the pacer pocket had eroded and was now infected. This is extremely dangerous, with the biggest fear being that the bacterial infection would work its way to the heart via the embedded pacer wires, causing what is referred to as Endocarditis.

This would require emergent high-dose antibiotics and surgical intervention. With all praise and glory to God, I was not nervous and actually felt at peace. I knew the Lord was with me, and I could feel his love and grace present.

My cardiologist, however, was feeling very nervous. In fact, it was the first time I had ever seen him pacing as he was talking to me, demanding my wife be contacted and present in the event decisions had to be made. Simply put, if I went into cardiac arrest, my cardiologist wanted her present to make "Do not resuscitate" and "Do not intubate" decisions on my behalf.

I understood his concern fully because, after all, two of the three pacer wires embedded had been in place for nearly 30 years. Naturally, they would be embedded within the muscle of my heart, causing great concern for tearing of the myocardium (heart muscle). There would also be a great concern for the damage of the heart valves as the wires were extracted.

Consequently, a thoracic surgeon was standing by if, while removing one or more of the wires, my myocardium would be torn and leak blood or exsanguinate, causing hypovolemic shock and death.

Here comes the miracle. Although the surgery lasted much longer than expected, upon completion, the pacemaker, including all wires, was successfully removed without any adverse reactions or conditions. There had been no damage to my myocardium or heart valves. Not only did I survive an infection involving the pacemaker site, but I came through the surgery without incident or complications. It was pretty cool.

Now, are you ready for this? Several days later, it was determined that I would no longer need a pacemaker. That's right, after nearly 30 years of depending on a pacemaker for survival, I now no longer require one." I saw Jean listening with utmost interest.

My heart rate was within normal limits and remained that way as I'm writing this book. All glory and praise to God!

"I would like to share with you three experiences I had, Jean. All three experiences revolved around evidence, miracles, and witnesses. Although I have faith with or without experiences, it is not surprising to me that faith experiences exist.

In my line of work, there is nothing better than an eyewitness. Some 15-plus years ago, while acting as a street provider, providing street medicine, I was dispatched to a reported cardiac arrest.

My partner and I arrived on location about 15 minutes after being dispatched. This female had now been in cardiac arrest for nearly 25 minutes. I quickly assess and aggressively start treating with advanced cardiac life support. She was intubated (breathing tube in the throat) and defibrillated. Fortunately, we were able to resuscitate her during transport with a successful outcome. Although rare with this kind of downtime, thankfully, it was a success.

Several days later, I was contacted by this lady's pastor, who provided an update on her condition. A few days later, I would meet her. To my surprise, what I thought was going to be a thank you for saving her life ended up being a very frustrated and angry woman. She was mad that she had been resuscitated. Honestly, this was a first for me.

She proceeded to tell me that while she was clinically dead, she had been to Heaven. She wanted to stay in Heaven, but we brought her back. Furthermore, she was further angered that she did not see her father's name in the Book of Life. She knew that he was not in Heaven. With tears in her eyes, she states, "My father did not believe in Jesus."

I was momentarily speechless. This is a woman who had been dead for 25 minutes before her resuscitation. Although she had no memory of the events leading up to her cardiac arrest, she knew every detail while she was dead. She remained depressed and angered for the next few weeks. She had a second cardiac arrest while in a rehabilitation facility. This time she remained in Heaven, a place where she longed to be.

"Jean, I had a great friend who was an Indian native. He was heavily involved in developing emergency medicine and establishing a prehospital emergency medical system. I was blessed to have the invitation and opportunity to travel to India on multiple occasions to teach physicians and nurses the American way of delivering medicine. We would teach Advanced Cardiac Life Support and Basic Trauma Life Support to multiple classes with multiple students." I told Jean.

Interestingly, many of the emergency departments I visited throughout our travels in southern India had the most advanced equipment within their system but, at the time, did not have any form of synchronized airway management or medication administration. Here in the states, we call it an algorithm. In the presence of acute myocardial infarction (heart attack) or cardiac arrest, we have a chain of events that are statistically proven ways of what to give, how much to give, and when to give it, better known as an algorithm.

While in India, my physician friend took me to a variety of historical spots, both urban and rural. Saint Thomas Mountain was one of the most meaningful spots he took me to. It was here that I saw the ancient wooden church, which still stands to this day. The Pope actually visited and spoke to the people in the 80's on this mountain top.

It was really meaningful to see where he stood as I envisioned the thousands of people that were there that day standing and sitting on the mountainside. I also saw the grave of Thomas the Disciple. One bone remains buried after grave robbers had removed most of his bones several years earlier.

Inside the church, behind the altar, is the bleeding heart of Disciple Thomas. As a large stone, it oozed red fluid, perceived to be blood up until around 200 years ago. It was so nice to have three of my crucifixes placed against the rock by the local nun and then returned to me.

We also visited the old city of Hyderabad, best known for its landmarks such as the Nizams Museum, which contains Nizams jewels. I was blown away by the beautiful jewels present, including one of the largest diamonds in the world, Jacob's Diamond. Another famous landmark within the old city is the Charminar. This is a four-pillared, beautiful structure built in 1591.

Not only does the Charminar hold historical value, but it is also religiously significant as well. The top floor contains a mosque. The Charminar was built by Muhammad Quli Qutb Shah and remains today. There are several theories as to why the Charminar was built. One is that the rains continued with massive flooding, so Shah promised God if He would make the rain stop, he would build the temple commonly known as the Charminar. However, most commonly known is that Shah constructed the Charminar to commemorate the eradication of cholera, a deadly disease that was widespread at the time. Upon the completion of construction, both ended.

As to evidence that solidified my faith, I would like to share with you three experiences I had. All three experiences revolved around evidence, miracles, and witnesses. Although I have faith with or without experiences, it is not surprising to me that faith experiences exist.

"So, you see, Jean. Faith comes easy to me. I have witnessed miracles and have seen evidence that would convince me beyond a shadow of a doubt that Jesus exists." "I see," Jean responds.

I want to leave you with something to consider. I know you need peace. I also know there's a part of you that wants to believe and have faith. I don't know, nor do I need to know, what sins you have committed in life. I do know that all sins are forgivable if you truly repent for these sins, remembering there is a difference between regret and repentance. Regret is when you're sorry you got caught. Repentance is when we are truly sorry for the action(s).

Only Jesus brings life out of death. Those that have little will have much. This is promised, Jean. Once we start to walk with Christ, we will shine with distinguishing characteristics that revolve around goodness. This is what sets us apart and makes us recognized by others. Once we surrender and accept Christ as our Savoir, the transformation will begin. Our spirit will be fed, leading to our hearts and mind being changed. If this interests you, I would like you to read this at a time of your convenience.

I handed Jean a piece of paper that I had written ahead of time for the perfect time. This was a perfect time. On the card were the following words:

"Father, I am a sinner in need of a Savior. Jesus, I believe that you are Lord. I surrender my life to you. I believe you were raised from the dead for the forgiveness of my sins. Jesus, I would ask that you come into my life and fill me with the Holy Spirit, keeping me free of sin. Satan, I rebuke you in the name of Jesus Christ my personal Savior who has all authority over me, now and forever. Amen."

I hope and pray that Jean will seek peace, understanding, and surrender to our Heavenly Father.

Chapter 13

ALL GOOD THINGS MUST END

02-20-2012, I received a telephone call. "Tom, Jean fell at home and fractured her hip. They also discovered she has acute leukemia."

"Oh no," I replied.

"She is in the local hospital."

02-24-2012, I knew this was a death sentence for Jean. At 92, a fractured hip is pretty much a lethal injury. With acute leukemia on top of this, it was very unlikely that Jean was leaving the hospital.

Upon arriving home, I talked to Cammy and explained that I had promised Jean she would meet my family. Cammy said, "Absolutely, we will get around."

Cammy, Dominic, Terence, and I went to the hospital.

Upon entering Jean's room, her face lit up like a Christmas tree. I introduced Cammy and the kids to her. Terence, our child with Downs, did something unexpected. He walked up to Jean, grabbed her hand, and kissed it. The following day he repeated this with another friend who died that same day. Never before had we seen him do this.

Jean told me she was at peace and ready. I choked up, trying not to cry in front of her. I was so relieved that she had surrendered, was at peace, and prepared to die.

After a lengthy visit, we got ready to leave. Jean pointed at Cammy, saying, "He's going to write a book about me." Cammy shook her head, affirming her statement. We said our final goodbyes, knowing that this would be the last time I would see her alive.

02-29-2012, I received a call at 23:34 advising that Jean had passed. The cause of death was Acute Renal Failure, Acute Leukemia, and Congestive Heart Failure.

03-07-2012, I had to keep my additional promise to Jean. I had to redress June and Jimmy in the morgue. This is something that I was not looking forward to, but I had to keep my promise.

After gowning up and putting on an N95 mask, June and Jimmy were pulled from the cooler. They were put on the table one at a time, with the promised dress attire being placed upon them.

June was draped with a blue nightgown, white socks placed on her feet, and a pair of slippers were in place. June was then placed in the body bag Jean had initially provided.

Next, Jimmy was placed on the table and dressed in a draped blue shirt, robe, and long blue insulated underwear draped tightly on his legs. Socks were placed on his feet along with slippers. Jimmy was placed in a separate body bag.

Both were now ready for transport to the cemetery to join Jean the next day.

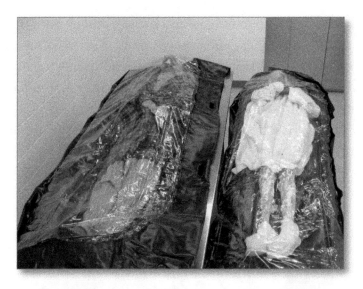

FIG. 29 JUNE AND JIMMY PREPARED FOR BURIAL.
PHOTO BY THOMAS M. CARMAN

03-08-2012 at 09:00, I transported June and Jimmy to the Lime Hill Cemetery. The funeral home met me there with Jean. She was wearing pink pajamas and a pink robe. Jean was in the same style body bag as June and Jimmy. At the cemetery, there was a large cement crypt. June was placed in the crypt first, with Kemp's headstone next to the crypt where he was buried. Jean was placed in the middle, with Jimmy next to Jean in the crypt. June, Jean, and Jimmy were placed on top of the mattresses Jean had in the building on her property. Under their heads, pillows were placed.

There were six of us present for the placement in the crypt. Additionally, two masonry gentlemen were awaiting in their truck to place the concrete top on the above-ground cement vault when we were finished.

Jean's neighbors, Mr. and Mrs. Franklin, were present. Mr. Franklin said a few words for Jean, and a small prayer was given. After, I waited for the cement lid to be placed on top of the vault. Now sealed forever, June, Jean, and Jimmy may rest in peace.

It is said that life is a book. Our chapters read as we would have them read. Each chapter represents periods of time within our life. Our activities, health, enjoyment, quality, and decision making. All of which are equally important, however, it is the last chapter that will define how we are remembered. More importantly, it is the last chapter that will define what library we will forever be displayed in, Heaven or hell.

FIG. 30 CEMENT CRYPT FOR JUNE, JEAN, AND JIMMY STEVENS.
PHOTO BY THOMAS M. CARMAN

To believe in the unseen can be extremely difficult. Faith is what sets us apart. When we hold onto faith, God will, in turn, use and redeem us.

If we're going to claim Christ, we must abide in the body of Christ because we are the body of Christ. We are the living flesh of Christ. Christ is no longer here in the flesh but is ever present in spirit, waiting upon our call.

Make no mistake about it; there is a lot of responsibility that comes with being a Christian. We should all strive to be Holy men and Holy women. This is no easy task in modern society. Thankfully, we have a Savior who died for our sins.

Tom Carman

Much like when we have an illness, we call upon a physician. In our daily life, we should call upon Christ. A physician prescribes medications, whereas Christ prescribes scriptures. Within these scriptures is the key to daily life.

Two years ago, I fully accepted Jesus Christ into my life, becoming born again. I went from being a believer to fully surrendering my life to Christ.

I credit some of this to Jean Stevens. At the time, neither Jean nor I knew how instrumental our chats and time spent together would be. As I spent increasing time in the scriptures, attempting to bring Jean to the point of peace and comfort, little did I know that I would find myself in need of this same peace and comfort several years later.

Jean is missed. I will never forget the lady who dug up her husband and twin sister. Her beautiful smile, quick wit, demands, and stubbornness will not soon be forgotten.

It took me nine years to get the courage to uphold my promise and write this book, but I'm sure she is looking down with that infamous smile on her face.

I remain without answers as to why Jean did what she did. At age 91, her actions were certainly unprecedented. Maybe it was love. Maybe it was claustrophobia. Maybe she didn't want to be forgotten.

As Haruki Murakami said, "Death is not the opposite of life, but a part of it."

Life is beautiful but unpredictable. When there is happiness, there is sorrow and loss too. Most people live without worries and forget the major part, which is death. However, there are many people who live with death in their minds; Sometimes, it could be good for you as it helps you live a good life just as God wants, but sometimes it could be the worst thing to happen to you because when a person is thinking about death all the time? He forgets to live in the present and spends his life worrying about the process and what might happen to him after death. This condition takes life and ev-

169

erything good from the person, making them hollow. The person is always on edge, worrying about his life and death and not living it.

Life will become easier if we accept the fact that death is inevitable, and at some point, in life, it will happen. Fearing death will do nothing but cause unwanted stress and anxiety in your life. There could be many people like Jean who fear death or have some other fears which might cause them to be scared of death or dying alone. However, you can't just expect your family or friends to die with you just because you are scared of doing anything alone. I think the situation might have been a little different if Jean and her sister June were made to face their fears instead of doing nothing, like self-exposure therapy. Many readers might creep out or think of Jean as some crazy old lady for what she did initially but what they don't know is how kind, amazing, gentle, beautiful, and nifty that woman was. Sometimes, people get stuck in situations that portray them as bad or crazy, and the same happens with Jean. They judge them by their mistakes and habits, and they did the same with Jean, including myself.

Now, as I sit in my house surrounded by my beautiful family, I still think about Jean. She was not just a case for me, but she was one of my great friends. Despite our differences and age gap and her being a gravedigger (She would have laughed if she heard it), we became friends, and I think this is beautiful about friendship. We don't care about race, religion, age, or face, but if we click with someone? It's for life. It was the same with Jean. Even after almost more than ten years, I wonder how my life could have been if I got to know why Jean did what she did, but I respect her reasons, and I just pray to God that she is in peace and happy up there with June and Jimmy, because I am happy and at peace.

Printed in the USA
CPSIA information can be obtained
at www.ICGtesting.com
LVHW020806110424
776968LV00015B/733